Shabbat Revolution

A Practical Guide
to Weekly Renewal

Shabbat Revolution

A Practical Guide to Weekly Renewal

Rabbi Elie Mischel

Edited by Shira Schechter
Cover and interior design by the Virtual Paintbrush

ISBN 978-1-957109-76-3 (hardcover)
ISBN 978-1-957109-75-6 (paperback)

First Edition 2025

www.Israel365.com

In Memory of

Tom Schiffour, z"l
"Rabbenu Tom"

(1945-2025)

It's been a long dark night were still waiting for the sun
It's hard to get some rest in a world that's on the run
When you think you're finished, you've only just begun
There's still work to be done

–Tom Schiffour, *Strengthen Your Hands*

Table of Contents

A World that Desperately Needs Shabbat

CHRISTIAN READER HOLDING a book about Shabbat, written by an Orthodox rabbi. Not long ago, this would have been unthinkable.

For nearly two thousand years, the relationship between Christians and Jews was marked by persecution, suspicion, and tragedy. Jews were cast as rejected by God, pressured to convert, expelled from countries, and worse. And yet, today, we are witnessing something extraordinary. Christians have become Israel's strongest supporters and the Jewish people's most steadfast friends.

This shift isn't just political. It's spiritual.[1]

The prophet Zechariah foresaw this moment when he wrote:

> "Thus says the Lord of hosts: In those days it shall come
> to pass that ten men from the nations of every tongue
> shall take hold of the corner of the garment of a Jew,

---

1   For a historical overview of the tension and reconciliation between Christians and Jews, see David Novak, *"Jewish-Christian Dialogue: A Jewish Justification"* (Oxford University Press, 1992).

saying, 'Let us go with you, for we have heard that God is with you'" (Zechariah 8:23).

Today, we see this prophecy fulfilled as Christians increasingly turn to Jewish sources not to change us, but to learn from us—seeking to understand the Hebrew roots of their faith and the deeper meanings of God's word. As an Orthodox rabbi, I do not take this friendship for granted. It is nothing less than a modern miracle, a testament to God's enduring faithfulness.

The Crisis of Our Time

Never has humanity been more in need of Shabbat's wisdom than today. We live in what sociologists call an "acceleration society,"[2] where the pace of life increases exponentially with each passing year. The very technologies that promised to liberate us have instead become our taskmasters, creating a state of permanent accessibility and endless productivity.

Consider the reality of modern life: The average office worker faces an avalanche of over one hundred emails daily, each one demanding attention and response. Our phones have become like appendages, with studies showing people checking them hundreds of times daily—approximately every four minutes of waking life. The traditional boundary between work and rest has crumbled, with nearly half of Americans regularly working on weekends. The cost of this relentless pace manifests not just in billions of dollars of stress-related healthcare expenses, but in the fragmenting of our families and communities.

But these observable patterns only hint at the deeper spiritual crisis we face. We are experiencing what philosophers call "time famine"—the perpetual feeling of never having enough time.[3]

---

2   Hartmut Rosa, *Social Acceleration: A New Theory of Modernity* (Columbia University Press, 2013).
3   Brigid Schulte, *Overwhelmed: Work, Love, and Play When No One Has the Time* (Sarah Crichton Books, 2014).

It's ironic: despite all our time-saving devices and productivity tools, we feel more rushed than ever before. Even our leisure has become a form of work as we "optimize" our workouts, "maximize" our vacations, and feel pressure to make every moment "count." We have lost the art of simply being.

King Solomon, the wisest of all men, warned us about this very phenomenon: "What profit has man of all his labor wherein he labors under the sun?" (Ecclesiastes 1:3). Despite all our technological advances, we still struggle with this fundamental question. We have gained extraordinary capabilities but lost our souls. We have conquered space through technology but lost our sense of sacred time. We are more connected than ever through social media, yet studies show we are lonelier than any previous generation.

The Bible teaches that after creating the universe, God rested on the seventh day, blessing it and making it holy (Genesis 2:3). This wasn't because God was tired; the Creator of the universe doesn't need rest. Rather, God was teaching humanity something fundamental: stopping is not a waste of time but rather its fulfillment. True creativity requires rhythm, a pattern of engagement and withdrawal, doing and being.

This crisis isn't just about being busy—it's about losing our humanity. When we never stop producing, acquiring, and achieving, we forget who we are beyond our roles and responsibilities. We forget what the prophet Isaiah meant when he said, "In returning and rest you shall be saved; in quietness and in confidence shall be your strength" (Isaiah 30:15).

Our generation desperately needs to rediscover the sacred art of stopping. We need to remember that we are human beings, not human doings. What we need is nothing short of a Shabbat Revolution—not just as a religious observance but as a sanctuary from the relentless demands of the marketplace and a source of restoration for our stressed and fragmented lives.

The Divine Answer: Shabbat

In the beginning, God created the heavens and the earth. For six days, He shaped existence itself through divine speech, bringing forth light and darkness, sea and dry land, all living creatures, and finally, humankind. Then, on the seventh day, something shocking occurred: "God completed His work which He had done, and He ceased on the seventh day from all His work which He had done. God blessed the seventh day and sanctified it, because on it He ceased from all His work which God created to make" (Genesis 2:2-3).

This divine pause was more than just a historical event. When God later gave the Bible to the people of Israel at Mount Sinai, He commanded us to observe this pattern for all generations: "Remember the Shabbat day to keep it holy" (Exodus 20:8). This remembrance is not merely a passive act of mental recall, but an active engagement with the rhythm of creation itself.

The Hebrew word for "ceased" used in Genesis is *vayishbot*, from which we derive the word "Shabbat." But this cessation was not mere idleness. Our sages teach that what God created on the seventh day was *menucha*—rest itself. This rest was not a negative state, the absence of work, but a positive creation, as real and vital as light or life. In the words of the ancient rabbis, "What was the world lacking? *Menucha*. When Shabbat came, *menucha* came."[4]

Rest is not a concession to weakness but the mark of completion. God didn't rest on the seventh day because He was weary—He rested to set a pattern for the world. True fulfillment isn't found in endless toil but in knowing when to pause. Creation reaches its highest point not in constant expansion, but in the wisdom to step back.

When God blessed and sanctified the seventh day, He infused time itself with holiness. Unlike the sacred spaces of the

---

4   Babylonian Talmud, Shabbat 10b

ancient world—temples, mountains, shrines—Shabbat is not bound to a place but woven into the fabric of time, accessible to all regardless of location or status. As Rabbi Abraham Joshua Heschel beautifully wrote, Shabbat is a "palace in time,"[5] a dimension of holiness we can enter every week.

The genius of Shabbat lies not just in its regular recurrence but in its comprehensive nature. It offers not just an interruption of our work, but a complete reordering of our relationship with time, possessions, and most importantly, with God Himself. The Jewish sages call Shabbat a "taste of the World to Come"[6]—a gift, not a burden. For one day each week, we are invited to cease our labor and manipulation of the physical world. We stop trying to change the world and instead appreciate it as it is, shifting from the realm of creation to the realm of relationship—with God, with each other, and with our own souls.

The command to *"remember"* Shabbat[7] carries special significance in Hebrew thought. The Hebrew word *zachor* implies more than mental recollection—it calls us to actively remember through deed. We are called to remember creation by becoming partners with the Creator, to remember the Exodus from Egypt by tasting freedom ourselves, to remember divine rest by creating spaces of holiness in our own lives.

This remembrance transforms us. In six days of creation, God spoke the world into being. But on the seventh day, God was silent—and in that silence, meaning emerged. Similarly, when we step back from our constant doing, speaking, and producing, we create space to hear the still, small voice that is so often drowned out by the noise of our lives.

God's answer to our modern crisis isn't a new technology or a productivity hack—it's the biblical pattern of Shabbat.

5   Rabbi Abraham Joshua Heschel, *"The Sabbath"* (Farrar, Straus and Giroux, 1951).
6   Babylonian Talmud, Berachot 57b
7   Exodus 20:8

What we need today is a Shabbat Revolution. As the Zionist thinker Ahad Ha'am put it, "More than the Jewish people have kept Shabbat, Shabbat has kept the Jewish people."[8] This same Shabbat can now keep our sanity in a world that's lost its way.

In a world that has forgotten how to rest, Shabbat isn't just a break—it's a return to wholeness. In a culture that measures worth by output, it declares that we are valued for who we are, not what we produce. In an age of endless distraction, it carves out space for the sacred.

The rhythm God set at creation was never meant to be a relic of the past. It is as urgent now as it was then. This is the heart of the Shabbat Revolution. When we step into this divine rhythm, we aren't just remembering creation—we are part of its ongoing renewal.

The Workings of Jewish Tradition: The Vessel and the Water

Before we explore the practical observance of Shabbat, it's crucial to understand something about Jewish tradition and its relationship to Scripture. Many readers are understandably wary of "tradition," concerned that human customs might supersede God's written word. Yet tradition, properly understood and applied, is essential to the Shabbat experience.

The relationship between the Bible and traditional observance is beautifully illustrated within the Bible itself. When God commands us to "remember the Shabbat day to keep it holy" (Exodus 20:8), He doesn't specify how to do so. When He tells us, "You shall teach [these words] diligently to your children" (Deuteronomy 6:7), He doesn't lay out a precise method. When He instructs us to "rest" on the seventh day, He doesn't define what constitutes work and what qualifies as rest. Again and again, the Bible provides guiding principles that require explanation and practical application.

---

8   Ahad Ha'am, *Shabbat and Zionism*, https://benyehuda.org/read/2786

Consider the command: "You shall dwell in booths for seven days" (Leviticus 23:42). What exactly qualifies as a booth? How tall must it be? What materials can be used? Can it have a canvas top? The Bible doesn't provide these details, yet they are essential to fulfilling the command. Judaism's oral tradition fills in these gaps, preserving teachings passed down from Moses and refined through careful analysis by the sages of each generation.

The same is true for another well-known command: "You shall write [these words] on the doorposts of your house" (Deuteronomy 6:9). What words should be written? How should they be inscribed? Where exactly should they be placed? The tradition provides the necessary guidance while remaining faithful to the biblical text.

Shabbat offers a powerful example. The Torah commands us to remember and sanctify the seventh day—but how do we do that in practice? Jewish tradition provides a concrete answer: *Kiddush*, a blessing recited over wine on Friday night, proclaims God's creation of the world and the sanctity of Shabbat. This transforms an abstract command into a living ritual. Similarly, while the Torah tells us to cease work on Shabbat, it doesn't fully define "work." Jewish tradition identifies 39 categories of creative labor, derived from the activities used to construct the Tabernacle, offering a clear and structured framework for observance.

At its heart, tradition acts as a vessel for the Divine, ensuring that biblical principles are lived out in meaningful ways. To understand this, consider the parable of the vessel and the water:

A man is desperately thirsty. Before him sits a pitcher of pure, crystal-clear water, but he has no cup. He tries to drink directly from the pitcher, but the water spills everywhere. The water is wasted, and his thirst remains unquenched. Meanwhile, another man has a beautiful cup but no water—equally useless for quenching thirst.

In this parable, the water represents spirituality—our soul's deep thirst for connection with God, while the cup represents Jewish law—the vessel that contains and preserves that spirituality. Without the framework of law, even the most exalted spiritual experiences eventually dissipate, like water spilling to the floor.

This is why Shabbat comes with many "don'ts": Orthodox Jews don't drive, use electronics, cook, write, or engage in commerce. These restrictions might seem limiting to an outside observer. But for those who observe them, they create a sacred space in time where deeper awareness becomes possible. When we can't drive anywhere, we appreciate where we are. When we can't check our phones, we notice who is actually with us. When we can't spend money, we remember that our worth isn't determined by what we own or produce.

The sages of the Talmud were acutely aware of the balance between tradition and Scripture. They carefully traced each practice to its biblical source, often through complex legal reasoning. Their goal was not to add to God's law but to understand and apply it fully. They taught us to "Make a fence around the Torah"[9]—to establish practices to help people observe the biblical commands properly.

This approach reflects a deep reverence for the text itself. The Bible's divine wisdom contains layers of meaning that reward careful study. The sages saw their role not as legislators creating new laws, but as students uncovering the Bible's deeper implications and applications.

The laws of Shabbat, then, are not arbitrary restrictions but a vessel that allows us to fully experience its transformative power. They create a sanctuary in time—a holy interval where we can truly rest, not just physically but spiritually.

This understanding can help readers appreciate the wisdom

---

9   Ethics of the Fathers 1:1

preserved in Jewish practice without feeling obligated to adopt it wholesale. The biblical command to rest one day in seven is universal; the specific ways Jewish tradition has developed to guard this rest can inspire and inform without binding those outside the covenant of Israel.

In the chapters that follow, we will explore both the biblical foundations and traditional expressions of Shabbat. Readers are invited to draw insight from both, discovering ways to honor Shabbat that resonate with their own faith journey.

A Gift for All: Not a Call to Convert

As an Orthodox rabbi writing about Shabbat for a primarily Christian audience, I am deeply aware of the delicate balance this book must strike. Some might wonder why a Jewish religious leader would write about Shabbat for those who are not obligated to observe it in the traditional Jewish way. Others might question whether learning about Jewish practices could somehow compromise their Christian faith.

These are valid questions that deserve honest answers. The prophet Isaiah envisions a time when "many peoples shall go and say: 'Come, Let us go up to the Mount of God, To the House of the God of Jacob; That we may be instructed in God's ways, And that we may walk in God's paths.' For instruction shall come forth from Zion, The word of God from Jerusalem" (Isaiah 2:3). Rabbi Meir Wisser offers a fascinating interpretation of these words, explaining that "God's ways" refers to the broader principles of faith, while "God's paths" refer to the detailed commandments and practices that flow from those principles. In the end days, the nations will not only seek to understand God's general teachings, but will also desire to incorporate the specific practices and detailed commandments into their lives.[10]

We are witnessing this prophecy unfold today in a remarkable

---

10 Rabbi Meir Wisser, Isaiah 2:3

way. Growing numbers of Christians, while remaining firmly committed to their faith, are embracing the biblical commandments in a way that would have been unthinkable in previous generations. They aren't just interested in abstract spiritual principles—they want to live out God's laws as expressed in the Bible. Nowhere is this more evident than in the growing Christian interest in Shabbat, as many seek to understand how this divine gift can deepen their walk with God.

This book is a response to numerous requests from Christian friends and leaders who want to better understand Shabbat— not to observe it exactly as Jews do, but to draw inspiration from its wisdom for their own relationship with God. God's love and wisdom extend to all humanity. Judaism teaches that while the Bible contains commandments specifically given to the Jewish people as part of our unique covenant with God, its principles offer guidance for all. Every person can cultivate a deep and meaningful connection with the Creator by living an ethical, God-centered life.

Understanding the delicate balance between inspiration and appropriation is essential as you develop your own Shabbat practice. Jewish tradition teaches that God gave specific commandments (*mitzvot*) to the Jewish people at Mount Sinai. When Jews fulfill these commandments, such as lighting Shabbat candles, they recite a blessing that includes the words "*asher kiddeshanu b'mitzvotav v'tzivanu*" — "who has sanctified us with His commandments and commanded us." In other words, Jews alone are commanded to fulfill these commandments, to the exclusion of the nations.

This doesn't mean that non-Jews are forbidden from embracing the gift of Shabbat. Rather, it means that while Jews observe these practices as divine obligations, others may choose to incorporate elements of Shabbat as an expression of free will and spiritual growth. This distinction is important - it allows us to respect the unique covenant between God and the Jewish people while recognizing that the principle of sacred rest is a universal gift embedded in creation itself.

When discussing the specific laws of Shabbat in this book, my intention is not to suggest that non-Jews must observe them. Instead, these teachings are shared because they reveal the deeper meaning of sacred time that can speak to anyone's spiritual journey. The relationship between understanding and practice is similar to appreciating classical music. If you want to deepen your appreciation for classical music, you might study how a great symphony orchestra functions—how the different instruments blend, how the conductor guides the ensemble, and how the music is structured. Even if you never join an orchestra, learning about these elements enhances your understanding and appreciation of the music.

Similarly, understanding how Jewish law structures Shabbat can offer valuable insights to anyone seeking meaningful weekly renewal. The specific "don'ts" of Shabbat—abstaining from driving, using electronics, cooking, writing, or engaging in commerce—create an environment where spiritual connection becomes possible. While Christians or others may observe their day of rest differently, the principles behind these practices offer universal wisdom for appreciating and experiencing holy time.

For instance, many non-Jews have discovered that voluntarily disconnecting from technology for twenty-four hours, sharing distraction-free meals with family, or refraining from commerce on their day of rest profoundly enhances their spiritual experience. These practices, while not obligatory, help carve out a sacred space for rest, renewal, and reconnection with God.

Judaism does not seek to convert others to its faith. We believe the righteous of all nations have a place in the World to Come, and that non-Jews are not obligated to follow Jewish law.[11] The purpose of this book is not to convince Christians to observe Shabbat as Jews do, but rather to share the deep wisdom God embedded in this weekly commandment—wisdom about rest, sacred time, and spiritual renewal.

Throughout this book, Hebrew terms and concepts will be explained in connection to their biblical roots, revealing how each practice directly fulfills God's commandments. You'll discover the wisdom embedded in Shabbat—wisdom that has sustained Jewish spiritual life through centuries of exile and return. Whether you seek to understand Jewish traditions or to deepen your own practice of weekly rest, the pages ahead contain practical insights drawn from thousands of years of lived experience. My hope is that by sharing this treasure of Jewish life with you, we will spark a true Shabbat Revolution and witness another step in the fulfillment of Zechariah's prophecy—Jews and Christians walking together in the light of the God of Abraham, Isaac, and Jacob.

---

11 According to Jewish tradition, non-Jews are obligated to observe the seven Noahide laws—prohibitions against idolatry, blasphemy, murder, theft, sexual immorality, eating flesh from a living animal, and establishing just courts—but are not required to follow the entirety of Jewish law.

Part One

A Practical Guide to Shabbat

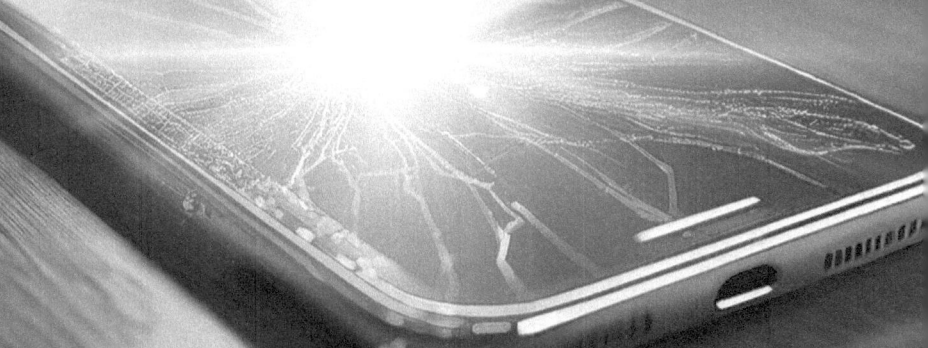

CHAPTER 1

Preparing for Shabbat

The Importance of Preparation

"Remember the Shabbat day to keep it holy" (Exodus 20:8). This divine commandment begins not on Shabbat itself, but in the days and hours leading up to it. The Hebrew word for "remember," *zachor*, implies active preparation - we must do something concrete to distinguish this day from all others. Just as a wedding requires careful planning to create a meaningful celebration, Shabbat demands thoughtful preparation to transform an ordinary day into sacred time.

In the desert, God Himself taught this lesson through the manna, the heavenly bread that sustained the Israelites. "On the sixth day they shall prepare what they bring in, and it shall be twice as much as they gather daily" (Exodus 16:5). Even in God's miraculous provision, preparation was required. The Israelites had to gather double portions on Friday to ensure they could rest on Shabbat. This wasn't just a practical measure, but a spiritual lesson: how we prepare shapes our experience of the sacred.

The Sages beautifully expressed this principle in their teaching: "One who toils on the eve of Shabbat will eat on Shabbat."[1] This goes far beyond merely preparing food, encompassing all the

---

1 Babylonian Talmud, Bava Metzia 83a

spiritual and practical preparations that transform Shabbat from a simple day of rest into what Isaiah calls "a delight" (Isaiah 58:13).

Throughout the Bible, we see that meaningful encounters with God require preparation. Before receiving the Ten Commandments, the Israelites spent three days preparing themselves (Exodus 19:10-11). Before entering the Tabernacle, the priests performed specific preparatory rituals (Exodus 30:17-21). These biblical patterns teach us that drawing close to God requires intentional preparation of both body and soul.

The preparations for Shabbat follow this biblical model. Like the careful preparations that went into the Tabernacle service, our Shabbat preparations create sacred space in both our homes and our hearts. Just as the priests needed to wash before entering the holy space, we prepare ourselves physically and spiritually for this holy time. When we invest effort in preparing for Shabbat, we demonstrate that we value this divine gift and understand its significance in our lives.

The very act of preparation itself begins to shift our consciousness from the mundane to the sacred. As we clean our homes, prepare special foods, and set aside our weekly concerns, we gradually transition from ordinary time into what will become, for twenty-five hours, a taste of eternity. These preparations are not mere rituals - they are the gateway to experiencing what the Bible calls "the Shabbat of the Lord" (Exodus 20:10).

Practical Steps: Cleaning, Cooking, and Setting the Stage

The physical environment we create affects our spiritual experience. When we transform our space from its everyday appearance to something special, we help ourselves and our families transition from mundane time to sacred time. This isn't about following specific rules, but about creating an atmosphere that supports rest, reflection, and spiritual connection.

Consider making your dining area a focal point of preparation. In Jewish homes, the table is transformed with a special tablecloth, the finest dishes, and often fresh flowers - not out of obligation, but to create beauty that honors God and lifts our spirits. Anyone can adopt similar practices that work for their family. A special tablecloth, place settings reserved for Shabbat, or other touches of beauty can help mark this time as different from the rest of the week. As the Psalmist writes, "In Your presence is fullness of joy" (Psalm 16:11). The preparations and atmosphere of the dining area on Shabbat reflect the deeper joy and connection found in God's presence.

The Hebrew word for honor, "*kavod*," shares its root with "*lechabed*" - to sweep or clean. This linguistic connection reveals something important about Shabbat preparation. Just as we sweep dust from our floors - matter that is external to the surface itself - our pre-Shabbat preparations invite us to sweep away the accumulated spiritual dust of our week. The sages teach that true *kavod*, true honor, comes from honoring others, or more deeply, from helping them clear away their own accumulated spiritual dust. When we prepare our homes and ourselves for Shabbat, we engage in this holy act of "*kavod Shabbat*" - honoring Shabbat by sweeping away the external layers to reveal our authentic selves and create space for genuine connection with others.

The goal isn't to create stress, but to establish simple practices that mark this time as special. Creating a beautiful, peaceful environment helps make your home a sanctuary for family gathering and spiritual renewal.

Food preparation offers another opportunity to make Shabbat special. While traditional Jewish homes follow specific laws about cooking before sunset, the principle behind these practices is universal: preparing food in advance allows everyone in the household to truly rest and enjoy fellowship together.

Consider preparing special meals that become Shabbat

traditions for your family. These don't need to be elaborate - what matters is that they're different from everyday meals and prepared with love and intention. The aroma of special foods cooking can help signal to everyone that sacred time is approaching. Some families enjoy baking bread together on Friday afternoon, while others prepare a meal that can cook slowly and fill the house with welcoming aromas.

The Book of Psalms tells us that God "satisfies the longing soul, and fills the hungry soul with goodness" (Psalm 107:9). Our physical preparations for Shabbat reflect this principle. By preparing special foods with intention and love, we create an environment where both body and soul can be nourished.

Remember that the goal of preparation isn't perfection. The ancient Jewish sages taught that while we should honor the Shabbat to the best of our ability, we shouldn't let anxiety about preparations overshadow the day's true purpose. Simple preparations done with love can create an atmosphere where true rest and spiritual renewal can flourish.

The Shabbat Wardrobe

When God prepared to give the Bible to the people of Israel at Mount Sinai, He instructed Moses to tell the people: "Consecrate themselves today and tomorrow. Let them wash their clothes and be ready by the third day" (Exodus 19:10-11). From this we learn that spiritual moments require physical preparation. Just as the Israelites prepared themselves to receive God's word, we prepare ourselves to receive the gift of Shabbat.

In Jewish homes around the world, family members take turns showering or bathing on Friday afternoon, a physical cleansing that represents spiritual renewal. Special clothes are laid out - clothes reserved for Shabbat and festivals. This change of clothing isn't about fashion but about marking the transition from ordinary to sacred time.

Many Jews maintain a special "Shabbat wardrobe." The way we dress affects how we feel and behave. When we dress with dignity, we're more likely to act with dignity. Special clothing helps create that elevated state of mind that Shabbat calls for.

Creating Sacred Atmosphere

The hour before Shabbat holds special significance. Jewish mystical tradition teaches that this time has unique spiritual potential. It's ideal to finish all preparations at least an hour before sunset, creating a buffer zone between the rush of preparation and the peace of Shabbat itself. As sunset approaches, the pace of preparation gradually shifts from hurried activity to peaceful anticipation. Work should ideally stop, giving everyone time to shower, change into special Shabbat clothes, and prepare mentally for the day ahead.

During this time, many families cultivate a serene atmosphere in their homes by playing traditional Shabbat melodies or spiritual music, reading Psalms together, or sharing words of inspiration, all to build a sense of anticipation for the Shabbat

Spiritual and Mental Preparation

Perhaps the most challenging aspect of Shabbat preparation in our modern world is the mental transition it requires. We live in an age of constant connectivity, where work and social obligations follow us everywhere through our devices. Preparing for Shabbat means learning to disengage, to create clear boundaries between sacred and ordinary time.

This fundamental connection between our weekday conduct and our Shabbat experience is beautifully captured by Rabbi Adin Steinsaltz: "Just as the food enjoyed on Shabbat has to be cooked beforehand, it does not just appear out of the sky, Shabbat is the time for enjoying what was prepared during the week. The awakening of delight is the result of the performance of *mitzvot* [commandments] during the previous days. Shabbat is not a free gift. The conclusion to be drawn from this is that whatever a person is during the week, he is the same on Shabbat. If a man behaves like a dog during the six days, he remains something of a dog on the seventh, except that he is now a Shabbat dog."[2] Shabbat preparation is not just about cooking and cleaning; it extends to the way we live our lives throughout the week. How we spend our time, how we treat others, and how we engage with our faith all contribute to the sanctity we experience on Shabbat.

The Bible tells us that even during the intense work of building the Tabernacle, all activity ceased for Shabbat. "Six days work shall be done, but on the seventh day you shall have a Shabbat of complete rest, holy to the Lord" (Exodus 35:2). If even the holy work of building God's sanctuary was suspended for Shabbat, surely we too can learn to set aside our urgent tasks.

Jewish tradition recommends completing all work well before sunset on Friday. This isn't just about finishing tasks - it's about clearing our minds to receive Shabbat properly. Many people find it helpful to review their week, tie up loose ends, and make peace with what remains undone. Some write notes about ongoing projects so they won't have to hold them in mind over Shabbat. Others take time for personal prayer or meditation.

A beautiful custom among traditional Jews is to study the weekly Torah portion on Friday afternoon. This helps shift our focus from worldly concerns to spiritual matters. As King David wrote, "The law of the Lord is perfect, refreshing the soul" (Psalm 19:7). It also prepares us for the public Torah reading that will take place in the synagogue the next morning.

A Word About Stress

It might seem ironic that preparing for a day of rest can sometimes feel overwhelming. Shopping, cooking, cleaning, and

---

2   Rabbi Adin Steinsaltz, *The Candle of God*, (Jason Aronson, 1998), 40.

organizing in advance can create a flurry of activity that feels contrary to the calm and peace Shabbat promises. But remember: Shabbat is not just about physical rest; it's about spiritually elevating the week. This requires intentional preparation and effort. By dedicating time and energy to Shabbat preparations, we transform our ordinary week into something sacred, setting the stage for a deeper connection to God, ourselves, and others.

However, the rush to prepare can sometimes lead to tension, especially within families. The Talmud tells of a couple who would have terrible fights each week before Shabbat. When the great sage Rabbi Meir visited their neighborhood, he spent three weeks helping them until he made peace between them. Afterward, he heard the voice of a prosecuting angel lamenting: "Woe is me, for Rabbi Meir has chased me out of this home."[3]

This story illustrates how easy it is to snap at a spouse or lose patience with children when the clock is ticking and tasks feel overwhelming. Ironically, this stress can undermine the very harmony that Shabbat is meant to bring. To avoid this, approach preparations with a spirit of teamwork and shared purpose. Delegate tasks to others when possible, and don't hesitate to involve children in age-appropriate ways. Even small contributions—like setting the table or choosing flowers—can foster a sense of ownership and joy.

When stress begins to rise, pause and take a deep breath. Remind yourself of the bigger picture: you're preparing not just a meal or a home but a sacred space for connection and renewal. Speak kindly to one another, and if an argument does arise, take a moment to apologize and reset. It's better to enter Shabbat with a little less done but a spirit of love and cooperation than with every detail perfect but relationships strained.

If you're new to Shabbat or rethinking your routine, start small. Focus on one or two aspects of preparation that feel

---

3   Babylonian Talmud, Gittin 52a

manageable and meaningful to you. Over time, you can build a rhythm that fits your life. A simple meal shared with loved ones, free from distractions, can be just as beautiful as an elaborate feast.

As you prepare, take to heart the words of the prophet: "Not by might, nor by power, but by My Spirit, says the Lord of hosts" (Zechariah 4:6). While it's important to do your part, remember that the essence of Shabbat—the holiness and peace it brings—is a divine gift. Our preparations are merely the vessel to receive this gift, transforming ordinary space and time into something extraordinary.

Finally, give yourself grace. Shabbat is not about achieving a perfect outcome but about setting aside time to connect with God, yourself, and those you love. Even if everything isn't completed or doesn't go exactly as planned, the spirit of Shabbat will still arrive. Allow its beauty to unfold naturally, and let its restfulness replenish your soul. As the sun begins to set on Friday evening, we let go of all our preparations, perfect or imperfect, and prepare our hearts to receive the Shabbat Queen. For ultimately, Shabbat's holiness does not depend on our efforts but on God's blessing, as it is written: "And God blessed the seventh day and made it holy" (Genesis 2:3).

CHAPTER 2

Friday Night Prayers - Welcoming the Sacred

Lighting the Shabbat Candles

As the sun begins to sink toward the horizon on Friday afternoon, Jewish women around the world perform one of Judaism's most powerful and transformative rituals: the lighting of the Shabbat candles. In homes everywhere, this lighting marks the official beginning of Shabbat, transforming an ordinary evening into a time of holiness and peace.

While anyone may light the candles, tradition gives precedence to women for this sacred task. The sages explain that since Eve, the first woman, diminished the world's light through her role in eating from the Tree of Knowledge, her daughters were given the privilege of bringing light back to the world each Friday at dusk.[1]

The sages teach that the gates of heaven are particularly open to women's prayers at this moment. Many women use these precious moments after lighting to pray for their families, their communities, and the world.

---

1   Midrash Tanchuma, Bereishit 9

Prayer after Lighting the Shabbat Candles

Yehi ratzon millefanecha, adonai elohai elohei yisra'el, shettechonein oti (ve'et ishi) ve'et kol kerovai, vetittein lanu chayyim tovim va'arukkim, vetizkereinu bezichron tovah uverachah, vetifkedeinu bifkuddat yeshu'ah verachamim, vetashkein shechinatecha beineinu, vezakkeinu legaddeil banim uvenei vanim chachamim unevonim ohavei adonai, yir'ei elohim, anshei emet zera kodesh, badonai deveikim ume'irim et ha'olam batorah uvema'asim tovim uvechol melechet avodat habborei. Anna, shema et techinnati bizchut sarah verivkah rachel velei'ah immoteinu, veha'eir nereinu shello yichbeh le'olam va'ed, veha'eir panecha venivvashei'ah. Amen.

English:

May it be Your will, O Lord my God and God of Israel, that You be gracious to me (and my spouse) and all my relatives, and grant us good and long lives. Remember us for good and blessing, and consider us for salvation and compassion. May Your Divine Presence dwell among us, and may we merit to raise children and grandchildren who are wise and understanding, who love the Lord and fear God, people of truth, holy offspring, who cling to the Lord and illuminate the world with Torah and good deeds and all the work of serving the Creator. Please, hear my supplication in the merit of Sarah, Rebecca, Rachel, and Leah, our mothers, and illuminate our light so that it never extinguishes forever and ever. May You shine Your face upon us and we shall be saved. Amen.

The timing of candle lighting holds deep significance. In accordance with the biblical command to "guard the Shabbat" (Deuteronomy 5:12), we light the candles shortly before sunset on Friday. This creates a buffer zone ensuring we don't accidentally violate the sanctity of the day by kindling fire after Shabbat has already begun. This practice formally begins Shabbat, which lasts for approximately 25 hours, from sunset on Friday evening until the appearance of three stars on Saturday evening.

In Jewish tradition, families light at least two Shabbat candles, though many add additional candles for each child. The two candles carry multiple layers of meaning. They represent the two versions of the Shabbat commandment in the Ten Commandments - "remember" (Exodus 20:8) and "guard" (Deuteronomy 5:12).[2] They also symbolize the dual aspect of Shabbat itself - the relationship between humans and God, and between human beings themselves.

The physical placement of the candles also carries significance. They are typically placed where they will be seen and enjoyed during the Friday night meal, on or near the dining room table. This placement reminds us that the light of Shabbat is meant to illuminate our relationships and enhance our joy. The candles transform our ordinary dining area into a sacred space, elevating our meal from mere eating to a spiritual experience.

When God began creation, His first spoken words were "Let there be light" (Genesis 1:3). Interestingly, this light was created before the sun, moon, and stars, which were not formed until the fourth day. The sages teach that this first light was different from physical light - it was a spiritual illumination through which one could see from one end of creation to the other. Though this primordial light was later hidden away for the righteous in the World to Come,[3] the Shabbat candles remind us of this original light, offering us a weekly glimpse of that pure illumination.

---

2   The two different versions of the Shabbat commandment appear in the Ten Commandments - *"Zachor"* (Remember) in Exodus 20:8 and *"Shamor"* (Guard or Observe) in Deuteronomy 5:12. The Babylonian Talmud (Shevuot 20b) teaches that these words were miraculously spoken simultaneously at Sinai.

3   Babylonian Talmud, Chagigah 12a

The lighting of the candles illuminates both the practical and spiritual dimensions of the day. On a practical level, the candles ensure that the home will be filled with light for the festive evening ahead. Spiritually, they represent the divine command "Let there be light" that began creation, as well as the light of peace and joy that Shabbat brings into our homes.

Jewish tradition teaches that the Shabbat candles bring *shalom bayit* (peace in the home). In ancient times before electricity, these candles prevented people from stumbling in the dark and arguing with each other. Today, even with electric lights, the soft glow of the Shabbat candles creates an atmosphere of tranquility and harmony that sets this evening apart from all others. The warm glow of the Shabbat candles transforms our homes into sacred spaces where we can truly experience the delight that Shabbat offers.

Lighting the Shabbat candles holds deep, universal significance. In the Bible, light symbolizes God's presence, wisdom, and peace. By lighting the candles, we mark the beginning of sacred time, creating a moment of spiritual clarity that has the power to transform our homes and our hearts.

This simple act also teaches us about spiritual transformation. We take ordinary wicks and candles, and with intention, turn them into symbols of holiness. In the same way, Shabbat takes the ordinary time of our week and elevates it into something sacred. The candles remind us of our ability to bring holiness into the physical world through spiritual awareness.

The light of the Shabbat candles also symbolizes hope. Just as a small flame can fill a dark room with light, our small acts of sanctification can brighten the world. The prophet Isaiah described Israel as "a light unto the nations" (Isaiah 49:6), and each Friday night, Jewish women around the world live out this calling, bringing light into their homes and, by extension, into the world.

Kabbalat Shabbat: A Mystical Welcome to the Shabbat Queen

High in the mountains of northern Israel, in the mystical city of Safed, a remarkable spiritual revolution took place in the 16th century. A circle of great Jewish mystics, led by Rabbi Isaac Luria, developed new forms of prayer and ritual that would transform Jewish spiritual life forever. Among their most enduring innovations was the ceremony of *Kabbalat Shabbat* - "Welcoming the Shabbat."

These mystics took literally the Talmud's description of Rabbi Chanina, who would wrap himself in his special garments before sunset on Friday and declare, "Come, let us go out to welcome the Shabbat Queen!" They would leave the confines of their synagogues and homes, walking out into the fields as the sun began to set. There, they would turn toward the west, toward the setting sun, and welcome Shabbat with song and dance.

Why the fields? The mystics found their inspiration in Isaac: "And Isaac went out to meditate in the field at eventide" (Genesis 24:63).[4] Stepping outside the usual environment allows for a fresh perspective, helping us to welcome Shabbat with a deeper awareness and connection. By going to the fields, the Kabbalists taught us that sometimes we must physically distance ourselves from the noise and busyness of life in order to spiritually receive the peace and sanctity of Shabbat.

The service these mystics created is a masterpiece of spiritual psychology. It begins with six psalms, corresponding to the six days of creation. As we recite each psalm, we progressively free ourselves from the concerns and constraints of that day's creation, while also expressing our deepest hopes for universal recognition of God.

Psalm 95 opens with "Come, let us sing unto the Lord," a call to leave our everyday consciousness and enter sacred time. The

---

4   The Hebrew word *"lasuach"* translated here as "meditate" has been interpreted by commentators as referring to prayer, based on Psalms 102:1.

psalm reminds us that God is "a great King above all powers," helping us put our worldly concerns in perspective.

Psalm 96 proclaims "Sing unto the Lord a new song," because each Shabbat offers the possibility of genuine renewal. Significantly, this psalm calls on "all the earth" to "sing unto the Lord," and commands us to "declare His glory among the nations." Here, at the very beginning of Shabbat, we pray for the day when all people will recognize the one true God.

Psalm 97 begins "The Lord reigns; let the earth rejoice," describing God's sovereignty over all forces of nature. The psalm declares that "all who serve graven images will be ashamed," looking forward to the time when all idolatry will cease and all humanity will worship the Creator.

Psalm 98, another "new song," focuses on God's salvation and justice, proclaiming that "all the ends of the earth have seen the salvation of our God." This universal vision is particularly appropriate for Shabbat, which recalls both Creation (in which all humanity was created in God's image) and the future Messianic era, when all people will know God.

Psalm 99 speaks of God's kingship and holiness, drawing us ever higher in spiritual consciousness.

Finally, Psalm 29 describes God's voice in nature: in thunder, in the breaking of cedars, in the shaking of mountains. The psalm ends with "May God give strength to His people; may God bless His people with peace." This completion of our spiritual preparation reminds us that when we observe Shabbat properly, we help bring peace not only to ourselves but to the entire world.

These psalms of universal redemption, which the prophets described as a time when "the earth shall be full of the knowledge of the Lord, as the waters cover the sea" (Isaiah 11:9), are perfectly suited to Shabbat. As we enter Shabbat, we pray for and envision this future time of universal peace and divine knowledge.

The emotional and spiritual peak of *Kabbalat Shabbat* comes with the singing of *"Lecha Dodi,"* composed by Rabbi Shlomo Alkabetz, one of the great mystics of Safed. This beloved poem, now sung in Jewish communities worldwide, weaves together biblical verses and mystical imagery to personify Shabbat as a bride and queen.

Its famous refrain declares: "Come, my beloved, to meet the bride. Let us welcome the presence of Shabbat."

The Hebrew word for "come" (*lecha*) shares its root with the word for "walking" (*halicha*). This is not a passive waiting but an active going forth to greet the Shabbat. Just as a groom goes forth to meet his bride under the wedding canopy, we actively go forth to meet the Shabbat.

The poem's nine stanzas take us on a journey through Israel's history and hope for the future. They speak of Jerusalem's restoration, of exile and redemption, of divine love and human longing. The mystical tradition teaches that Shabbat itself is a taste of the World to Come, and in singing *Lecha Dodi*, we experience a foretaste of that ultimate redemption.

At the final verse, the entire congregation turns toward the entrance and bows to welcome the Shabbat Queen:

"Come in peace, crown of God, come with joy and cheerfulness; amidst the faithful of the chosen people come O bride; come, O bride."

This physical turning is intentional. We literally turn our backs on the week behind us and face the holiness that approaches. The bowing acknowledges that we are in the presence of royalty - not earthly royalty, but the sovereignty of sacred time itself.

The Lecha Dodi Prayer:

L'cha dodi likrat kala, p'nei Shabbat n'kab'lah!

Shamor v'zachor b'dibur echad, Hishmi'anu el ha'meyuchad.
Adonai echad u'shmo echad; L'shem ul'tiferet v'l'tehila.

L'cha dodi likrat kala, p'nei Shabbat n'kab'lah

Likrat Shabbat l'chu v'nelcha, Ki hi m'kor ha'bracha.
Me'rosh mi'kedem n'sucha; Sof ma'aseh b'mach'shava t'chila.

L'cha dodi likrat kala, p'nei Shabbat n'kab'lah

Mikdash melech, ir m'lucha, Kumi, tze'i mi'toch ha'hafecha.
Rav lach shevet b'emek ha'bacha; V'hu yachmol alai'yich chemla.

L'cha dodi likrat kala, p'nei Shabbat n'kab'lah

Hitna'ari me'afar kumi, Livshi bigdei tifartech ami. Al yad ben
Yishai beit haLachmi; Karva el nafshi g'ala.

L'cha dodi likrat kala, p'nei Shabbat n'kab'lah

Hit'oreri, hit'oreri, Ki va orech, kumi ohri. Uri, uri, shir daberi;
K'vod Adonai alai'yich nigla.

L'cha dodi likrat kala, p'nei Shabbat n'kab'lah

Lo tevoshi ve'lo tikal'mi, mah tishtochachi umah tehemi,
bach yechesu ani'ei ami, venivnetah ir al tilah.

L'cha dodi likrat kala, p'nei Shabbat n'kab'lah

Vehayu lim'shisah shos'ayich, verachaku kol miv'alayich, yasis
alaich Elohaich, kimesos chatan al kalah.

L'cha dodi likrat kala, p'nei Shabbat n'kab'lah

Yamin usmol tif'rotzi, ve'et Adonai ta'aritzi, al yad ish bein
partzi, venis'mechah venagilah.

L'cha dodi likrat kala, p'nei Shabbat n'kab'lah

Bo'ee v'shalom, ateret ba'ala, Gam b'simcha uv' tzhala.
Toch emunei am segula; Bo'ee chala, bo'ee chala.

L'cha dodi likrat kala, p'nei Shabbat n'kab'lah!

English:

Come, my friend, to meet the bride; let us welcome the Shabbat.

"Observe" and "Remember," in a single command, the One
God announced to us. The Lord is One, and his name is One,
for fame, for glory and for praise.

Come, my friend, to meet the bride; let us welcome the Shabbat.

Come, let us go to meet the Shabbat, for it is a source of
blessing. From the very beginning it was ordained; last in
creation, first in God's plan.

Come, my friend, to meet the bride; let us welcome the Shabbat.

Shrine of the King, royal city, arise! Come forth from thy
ruins. Long enough have you dwelt in the vale of tears!

He will show you abundant mercy.

Come, my friend, to meet the bride; let us welcome the Shabbat.

Shake off your dust, arise! Put on your glorious garments, my people, and pray: "Be near to my soul, and redeem it through the son of Jesse, the Bethlehemite."

Come, my friend, to meet the bride; let us welcome the Shabbat.

Bestir yourself, bestir yourself, for your light has come; arise and shine! Awake, awake, utter a song; the Lord's glory is revealed upon you.

Come, my friend, to meet the bride; let us welcome the Shabbat.

Be not ashamed nor confounded. Why are you downcast? Why do you moan? The afflicted of my people will be sheltered within you; the city shall be rebuilt on its ancient site.

Come, my friend, to meet the bride; let us welcome the Shabbat.

Those who despoiled you shall become a spoil, and all who would devour you shall be far away. Your God will rejoice over you as a bridegroom rejoices over his bride.

Come, my friend, to meet the bride; let us welcome the Shabbat.

You shall extend to the right and to the left, and you shall revere the Lord. Through the advent of a descendant of Perez we shall rejoice and exult.

Come, my friend, to meet the bride; let us welcome the Shabbat.

Come in peace, crown of God, come with joy and cheerfuln
ess; amidst the faithful of the chosen people come O bride;
come, O bride.

Come, my friend, to meet the bride; let us welcome the Shabbat.

 Scan Here to Hear this Prayer:
https://www.youtube.com/watch?v=WuEC4tvBXOo

Psalm 92: Seeing with Shabbat Eyes

The service culminates with Psalm 92, which bears the unique inscription "A Song for Shabbat Day." This is the only psalm in the entire Bible explicitly dedicated to Shabbat, and Jewish tradition teaches that at the moment we recite it, we formally welcome Shabbat into our lives. Yet something seems puzzling: after its opening dedication to Shabbat, the psalm appears to have nothing to do with the day of rest. Instead, it speaks of divine justice, the flourishing of the righteous, and the ultimate downfall of evildoers. What makes this "A Song for Shabbat Day"?

The answer lies in understanding what Shabbat offers us: not just physical rest, but a different way of seeing reality. During the six days of the week, we are immersed in the world of surface appearances. We see the wicked prosper while the righteous suffer. We witness injustice seemingly go unpunished. As the psalm itself says, "A brutish man does not know, neither does a fool understand this" (Psalms 92:7). From our limited weekday perspective, it's easy to question whether God is truly in control, or whether justice will ever prevail.

But Shabbat grants us what the Jewish mystics call "*chazon*"

- prophetic vision, the ability to see beyond surface appearances to deeper truth. One day a week, we step back from our usual activities and perspectives. Free from the distractions of commerce and technology, no longer caught up in the rush to achieve and acquire, we can finally see with clarity. The psalm expresses this transformative vision: "When the wicked spring up like grass, and when all the workers of iniquity flourish, it is that they may be destroyed forever" (Psalms 92:8).

This is the "Shabbat perspective" that the psalm teaches. Just as children might question a parent's actions because they cannot see the longer-term purpose, we often fail to understand God's management of the world because we see only fragments of the larger picture. But on Shabbat, we're granted a glimpse of the divine perspective. We begin to understand that what appears as random or unjust is part of a larger pattern of perfect justice that unfolds across time.

"The righteous shall flourish like the palm tree; he shall grow like a cedar in Lebanon" (Psalms 92:13). A palm tree grows slowly but steadily, remaining green and fruitful even in harsh conditions. Unlike grass, which springs up quickly but withers just as fast, the palm represents enduring growth and lasting achievement. This is what we can see on Shabbat - that true success is not measured in quick profits or immediate results, but in steady spiritual growth and lasting impact.

The psalm concludes with an especially powerful image: "They shall still bring forth fruit in old age; they shall be fat and flourishing." From a worldly perspective, old age represents decline and diminishment. But with Shabbat vision, we can see that spiritual achievements actually increase with age. Every commandment performed, every act of kindness, every moment of Bible study - these continue to bear fruit and influence the world long after they're performed.

This explains why this particular psalm introduces Shabbat.

As we prepare to enter the holy day, we need to adjust our spiritual vision. We're about to enter a dimension where time itself operates differently, where we can look past the confusing surface of events to their true meaning. The psalm trains us to see with clarity, teaching us about divine justice—that in the end, God will defeat evil and reward the righteous.

When we recite "A Song for Shabbat Day," we're not just singing about Shabbat - we're actively participating in its transformative power. We're declaring our readiness to see the world through Shabbat eyes, to perceive the divine justice and purpose that underlies all of creation. This is why Jewish tradition teaches that at this moment, an additional "soul of Shabbat" - the enhanced spiritual consciousness that characterizes the day - enters us.

Sing the Song of Shabbat

This moving song expresses how all of creation, from the stars to the trees, yearns to sing the song of Shabbat. It begins with the words of Psalm 92 in Hebrew, "A song for Shabbat day," and then continues in English, powerfully connecting this universal longing to the Jewish people's particular experience of maintaining faith even in humanity's darkest moments.

Mizmor shir l'yom hashabbat (A Song for Shabbat day),
Mizmor shir l'yom hashabbat (A Song for Shabbat day).

The whole world is waiting to sing the song of Shabbat,
The whole world is waiting to sing the song of Shabbat.

 Scan Here to Hear this Prayer:
https://www.youtube.com/watch?v=ijREaXKsouw

The mystics of Safed crafted a powerful weekly ritual—an intentional practice that transformed ordinary consciousness into a sacred one. While we may not go out into the fields to welcome Shabbat as they did, the essence of their practice still holds deep significance for us today.

Ma'ariv: The Evening Service

After welcoming Shabbat through *Kabbalat Shabbat*, we begin *Ma'ariv*, the evening service. While *Kabbalat Shabbat* was created by mystics in the 16th century, *Ma'ariv's* basic structure dates back to the Men of the Great Assembly[5] over two thousand years ago. The service takes on special significance on Friday night, with additional prayers celebrating Shabbat woven into its traditional framework.

The service opens with the *Barchu*, the formal call to prayer, where the prayer leader calls out "Bless the Lord, the Blessed One" and the congregation responds "Blessed is the Lord, the Blessed One, forever and ever." This responsive reading creates a sense of community and shared purpose as we begin our prayers.

Then comes a profound blessing about evening, praising God for ordering the cycles of time: "Blessed are You, Lord our God, King of the universe, who by His word brings on evenings, by His wisdom opens the gates of heaven, with understanding changes times and alternates the seasons... Who rolls away the light before the darkness and the darkness before the light... Blessed are You, Lord, who brings on evenings."

This blessing carries special meaning on Shabbat eve, as we witness the transition from weekday to holy day, from mundane time to sacred time. The imagery of God rolling away light before darkness and darkness before light reminds us that all

---

5   The Men of the Great Assembly, or *Anshei Knesset HaGedolah*, was a body of 120 sages who led the Jewish people in the early Second Temple period (circa 515 BCE - 70 CE). Their role in establishing prayers is discussed in Babylonian Talmud, Berachot 33a.

changes, even the most dramatic, are under divine control. Just as we can trust God to bring each evening and morning in its proper time, we can trust that our transition into Shabbat holiness is part of His divine plan.

The second blessing speaks of God's eternal love for the Jewish people, expressed primarily through the gift of Torah: "With eternal love You have loved Your people Israel, teaching us Torah and commandments, statutes and laws. Therefore, Lord our God, when we lie down and when we rise up, we will speak of Your laws and rejoice in the words of Your Torah and commandments forever. For they are our life and the length of our days; we will meditate on them day and night. May You never remove Your love from us. Blessed are You, Lord, who loves His people Israel."

This blessing carries special resonance on Shabbat evening. Throughout the week, our engagement with the Bible and divine wisdom is often hurried and fragmented, squeezed between work obligations and daily responsibilities. But Shabbat creates the space for deep Bible study and contemplation. The blessing reminds us that God's love is expressed not only through the gift of rest, but through the gift of divine teaching that gives meaning to our rest.

After these preparatory blessings, we reach the Shema itself.

The Shema: Declaring God's Unity at Twilight

The *Shema* is Judaism's central declaration of faith, recited every morning and evening in fulfillment of the biblical command: "You shall speak of these words... when you lie down and when you rise up" (Deuteronomy 6:7). While the *Shema* is always powerful, it takes on special significance during the Friday evening *Ma'ariv* service as we welcome Shabbat. Just as Shabbat testifies to God's creation of the world, the *Shema* testifies to His unity and continuing sovereignty over all creation.

The sequence of the Friday evening prayers leads us beautifully to this moment. First, we acknowledge God's control over nature in the evening blessing, watching as He "brings on the evening" and transforms day into night. Then we recognize His love as expressed through the Torah in the second blessing. Only then do we proclaim His unity in the *Shema*, having witnessed both His mastery over creation and His loving guidance through the Torah.

The first paragraph of *Shema* commands us to love God "with all your heart, with all your soul, and with all your might." As we enter Shabbat, freed from worldly distractions, we can finally direct our hearts fully toward God. The commandment to speak of God's words "when you sit in your house" becomes even more meaningful as we look forward to the simple, beautiful moments of Shabbat—sharing meals and studying the Bible at home with those we love.

The second paragraph reminds us that Shabbat itself bridges the spiritual and physical worlds. Just as this passage connects our devotion to God with the physical blessings of rain and abundance, we honor Shabbat both through prayer and physical pleasures like festive meals. This paragraph's warning against being "led astray by your heart and eyes" resonates particularly on Shabbat eve, as we prepare to spend a day focused on higher purposes rather than material pursuits.

The third paragraph concludes by recalling the Exodus from Egypt - a theme that will appear again in our evening *Kiddush* (sanctification of the day over a cup of wine), linking Shabbat both to creation and to our liberation from slavery. As we recite these words on Friday evening, we prepare to enter a time of true freedom - freedom from mundane concerns and the opportunity to experience the deepest kind of liberty: the liberty to serve God.

The mystics teach that on Shabbat, the upper and lower

worlds are unified, making Friday evening an especially power-ful time for declaring God's unity through the *Shema*. We cover our eyes while saying the first verse, as we do every time we recite the *Shema* prayer, to block out all physical distractions at this transformative moment when weekday becomes a holy day.

Shema Yisrael

Shema Yisrael, Adonai Eloheinu, Adonai Echad.
Hear, O Israel: The Lord is our God, the Lord is One.

Baruch shem kevod malchuto le'olam va'ed.
Blessed be the name of His glorious kingdom for ever and ever.

First Paragraph of Shema

Ve'ahavta et Adonai Elohecha bechol levavecha uvechol nafshecha uvechol me'odecha. Vehayu hadevarim ha'eileh asher anochi metzavecha hayom al levavecha. Veshinantam levanecha vedibarta bam beshivtecha beveitecha uvelechtecha vaderech uvshochbecha uvekumecha. Ukshartam le'ot al yadecha vehayu letotafot bein einecha. Uchtavtam al mezuzot beitecha uvish'arecha.

And you shall love the Lord your God with all your heart and with all your soul and with all your might. And these words which I command you today shall be upon your heart. And you shall teach them diligently to your children, and you shall speak of them when you sit in your house and when you walk on the way, when you lie down and when you rise up. And you shall bind them as a sign upon your hand, and they shall be for frontlets between your eyes. And you shall write them upon the doorposts of your house and upon your gates.

Second Paragraph of Shema

Vehaya im shamoa tishme'u el mitzvotai asher anochi metzaveh etchem hayom le'ahava et Adonai Eloheichem ul'ovdo bechol levavchem uvechol nafshechem. Venatati metar artzechem be'ito yoreh umalkosh ve'asafta deganecha vetiroshcha veyitzharecha. Venatati esev besadcha livhemtecha ve'achalta vesava'ta. Hishameru lachem pen yifteh levavchem vesartem va'avadtem elohim acheirim vehishtachavitem lahem. Vechara af Adonai bachem ve'atzar et hashamayim velo yihyeh matar veha'adamah lo titen et yevulah va'avadtem mehera me'al ha'aretz hatovah asher Adonai noten lachem. Vesamtem et devarai eileh al levavchem ve'al nafshechem ukshartem otam le'ot al yedchem vehayu letotafot bein eineichem. Velimadtem otam et beneichem ledaber bam beshivtecha beveitecha uvelechtecha vaderech uvshochbecha uvekumecha. Uchtavtam al mezuzot beitecha uvish'arecha. Lema'an yirbu yemeichem vimei veneichem al ha'adamah asher nishba Adonai la'avoteichem latet lahem kimei hashamayim al ha'aretz.

And it shall come to pass ,if you surely listen to My commandments which I command you today ,to love the Lord your God and to serve Him with all your heart and with all your soul ,that I will give rain for your land at the proper time ,the early rain and the late rain ,and you will gather in your grain ,your wine and your oil .And I will give grass in your fields for your cattle ,and you will eat and be satisfied .Take care lest your heart be deceived and you turn and serve other gods and bow down to them. For then the Lord's wrath will flare against you ,and He will close the heavens and there will be no rain ,and the earth will not give its produce ,and you will perish quickly from the good land that the Lord gives you .And you shall place these words of Mine upon your heart and upon your soul ,and bind them as a sign upon your hand ,and they shall be for frontlets between your eyes .And you shall teach them to your children ,speaking of them when you sit in your house and when you walk on the way ,when you lie down and when you rise up .And you shall write them upon the doorposts of your house and upon your gates .In order that your days and the days of your children may be prolonged upon the land which the Lord swore to give to your fathers ,as the days of heaven over the earth.

Third Paragraph of Shema

Vayomer Adonai el Moshe leimor. Daber el benei Yisrael ve'amarta aleihem ve'asu lahem tzitzit al kanfei vigdeihem ledorotam venatenu al tzitzit hakanaf petil techelet. Vehaya lachem letzitzit ur'item oto uzchartem et kol mitzvot Adonai va'asitem otam velo taturu acharei levavchem ve'acharei eineichem asher atem zonim achareihem. Lema'an tizkeru va'asitem et kol mitzvotai vihyitem kedoshim l'Eloheichem. Ani Adonai Eloheichem asher hotzeiti etchem me'eretz Mitzrayim lihyot lachem l'Elohim ani Adonai Eloheichem.

And the Lord spoke to Moses, saying: Speak to the children of Israel and tell them to make fringes on the corners of their gar-ments throughout their generations, and to put a blue thread on the corner fringe. And it shall be for you as a fringe, that you may look upon it and remember all the commandments of the Lord and do them, and not follow after your heart and your eyes which lead you astray. In order that you remember and do all My commandments and be holy to your God. I am the Lord your God who brought you out of the land of Egypt to be your God; I am the Lord your God.

The Evening Amidah for Shabbat

The heart of every Jewish prayer service is the *Amidah*, recited while standing in silent devotion. On Shabbat, the central blessings of the *Amidah* prayer, unique to the holy day, beautifully capture the essence of Shabbat. The central blessing of the Friday night *Amidah* prayer weaves together themes from Genesis with personal petition, connecting our individual observance of Shabbat with God's original blessing of the seventh day.

The Sages teach that when we recite these verses, we join with God in affirming the story of creation. We echo God's own testimony about making the world in six days and resting on the seventh.

We end the blessing with the hope that God will be "pleased with our rest," and ask that He bless us with goodness, salvation and purity.

Ata Kidashta : You have Sanctified the Shabbat Day

Atah kidashta et yom hashvi'i lishmecha tachlit ma'aseh shamayim va'aretz, uveirachto mikol hayamim v'kidashto mikol hazmanim, v'chen katuv b'toratecha:

Vay'chulu hashamayim v'ha'aretz v'chol tz'va'am. Vay'chal Elohim bayom hashvi'i m'lachto asher asah, vayishbot bayom hashvi'i mikol m'lachto asher asah. Vay'varech Elohim et yom hashvi'i vay'kadeish oto, ki vo shavat mikol m'lachto asher bara Elohim la'asot.

Eloheinu veilohei avoteinu, r'tzei vimnuchateinu. Kad'sheinu b'mitzvotecha v'tein chelkeinu b'toratecha, sab'einu mituvecha v'sam'cheinu bishuatecha, v'taher libeinu l'ovd'cha be'emet. V'hanchileinu Adonai Eloheinu b'ahavah uv'ratzon Shabbat kodshecha, v'yanuchu vah Yisrael m'kad'shei sh'mecha. Baruch atah Adonai, m'kadeish haShabbat.

English:

You sanctified the seventh day for Your name's sake, as the culmination of the creation of heaven and earth. You blessed it above all other days, and sanctified it beyond other times, as it is written in Your Torah:

"The heavens and the earth were finished, and all their array. On the seventh day God completed His work which He had done, and He ceased on the seventh day from all His work which He had done. God blessed the seventh day and declared it holy, because on it He ceased from all His work which God had created to make" (Genesis 2:1-3).

Our God and God of our ancestors, be pleased with our rest. Sanctify us with Your commandments, grant us our portion in Your Torah, satisfy us with Your goodness, and gladden us with Your salvation. Purify our hearts to serve You in truth. In Your love and favor, Lord our God, grant us Your holy Shabbat as a heritage, and may Israel, who sanctifies Your name, rest thereon. Blessed are You, Lord, who sanctifies the Shabbat.

The Conclusion of Ma'ariv

The service concludes with a prayer that captures one of the most profound paradoxes of faith - how God can be both infinite and intimate at the same time. Known as *Magen Avot*, Shield of our Ancestors, this prayer begins by describing God's cosmic power: "Shield of our ancestors with His word, reviving the dead with His command, the holy God to whom none can compare."

Yet in the very same breath, this prayer describes the One who revives the dead as the same One who watched over

Abraham, Isaac and Jacob. God knows each of us personally, cares about our individual lives, and gave us the precious gift of Shabbat as a weekly reminder of His love. He is both the Master of the universe and the loving Father who gives His children a day of rest, both the Creator of infinite space and the Giver of sacred time.

This is why *Magen Avot* is so moving, for it reminds us that no matter how vast the universe may be, we are never lost in it. No wonder we end our Friday evening service with these words - they capture both the awesome majesty and the tender intimacy of our relationship with the Creator.

As *Ma'ariv* concludes, the transformation from weekday to Shabbat is complete. Through the power of these ancient prayers, we have shifted our consciousness from mundane concerns to sacred awareness. We are now ready to return home and continue our Shabbat celebration around the dinner table.

Magen Avot: Shield of our Ancestors

Magen avot bidvaro, m'chayei meitim b'ma'amaro, ha'El hakadosh she'ein kamohu, hameni'ach l'amo b'yom Shabbat kodsho, ki vam ratzah l'hani'ach lahem; l'fanav na'avod b'yirah vafachad, v'nodeh lishmo b'chol yom tamid, me'ein hab'rachot, El hahodaot, Adon hashalom, m'kadeish haShabbat um'vareich sh'vi'i umeni'ach bikdushah l'am m'dushnei oneg, zeicher l'ma'asei v'reishit.

English:

Shield of our ancestors with His word, reviving the dead with His command, the holy God to whom none can compare, who gives His people rest on His holy Shabbat, for in them He took delight to give them rest. Before Him we shall worship with reverence and awe, and give thanks to His name each day continually, Source of blessings, Lord of peace, who sanctifies the Shabbat and blesses the seventh day, and in holiness gives rest to a people filled with delight, a remembrance of the work of Creation.

 Scan Here to Hear this Prayer:
https://www.youtube.com/watch?v=tZsHcdhdPSo

CHAPTER 3

The Friday Night Meal

"**Y**EARS AGO, WHEN I would walk through the city on Friday nights, I would hear voices drifting from the windows of Jewish homes—here, the sound of *Kiddush*; there, the chanting of Psalms; elsewhere, the study of weekly Torah portion; from another the voice of a father testing his child in the Bible text he learned in school, echoing from a back room. All these sacred voices, melodies, and words seemed to rise together into the heavens, merging into a single harmony—like a symphony where each musician plays a different part, yet one unified song emerges. From every home in Israel, it was as if one song to God was rising—like the song of the Levites in the Holy Temple."[1]

Setting the Table: Creating a Sacred Space

In the Bible, we find a fascinating parallel between two types of sanctity. The first is the Tabernacle, where God commanded

---

1   Rabbi Kalonymus Kalman Shapira, *Derech HaMelech*, Sermons from Shabbat Shuva. Rabbi Shapira (1889-1943), known as the Piaseczner Rebbe, was a leading rabbi in the Warsaw Ghetto whose theological writings miraculously survived the Holocaust despite his murder by the Nazis in November 1943. An innovative Hasidic leader who established a significant yeshivah in Warsaw after World War I, he participated actively in Orthodox Jewish political life and maintained ties to the Land of Israel where his brother had settled as part of the religious Zionist movement.

Moses: "They shall make Me a sanctuary, that I may dwell among them" (Exodus 25:8).[2] The second is Shabbat itself, which God calls "My holy day" (Isaiah 58:13). Our sages teach that just as the Tabernacle was a sanctuary in space, Shabbat is a sanctuary in time.

The Friday night table becomes the meeting point of these two sanctuaries. Just as the priests prepared the Tabernacle with great care and attention to detail, we prepare our homes to become a *mikdash me'at* - a small sanctuary. Our sages explain that in the absence of the Temple in Jerusalem, our dining room tables take on the spiritual role of the Temple altar.[3]

The table is covered with a clean white tablecloth, symbolizing purity and sanctity, and two *challahs* (special loaves of bread eaten on Shabbat) are placed on top. These two loaves remind us of the double portion of manna that fell on Friday for use on Shabbat. They are kept covered until the blessing is made, teaching us sensitivity - we cover the bread so it won't be "embarrassed" while we first sanctify the day over wine. Even this small detail reminds us that creating sacred space involves attention not just to physical beauty but to spiritual refinement.

Before the *challah* is eaten it will be dipped in salt. This tradition is rooted in the biblical command that "on all your offerings you shall offer salt" (Leviticus 2:13). Just as salt was an essential component of the sacrifices in the Temple, it remains a symbolic reminder of the eternal covenant between God and Israel. It also teaches us an essential lesson: salt preserves and enhances flavor, just as Shabbat preserves and enhances our connection to holiness. In this way, the simple act of salting the bread transforms our meal into something sacred, linking us to the ancient Temple service.

Every element on the Shabbat table carries meaning. The table

---

2   This verse establishes the biblical commandment to build the Tabernacle, which later became the model for sanctifying space in Jewish tradition.
3   Babylonian Talmud, Chagigah 27a

itself represents the altar, and the white tablecloth evokes purity and sanctity. The challah symbolizes the double portion of manna that sustained the Israelites in the desert, while the salt sprinkled on it recalls the sacrificial offerings. Enhancing the Shabbat table is not about extravagance but about honoring the day, fulfilling the commandment to take joy in it. Whether through fine silverware, a carefully set table, or even simple yet thoughtful touches, these details transform the ordinary into something sacred.

Blessing the Children: A Sacred Moment of Connection

Of all the beautiful rituals that grace the Shabbat table, perhaps none is more moving than the blessing of children. This moment creates a weekly opportunity for parents to transmit love, values, and spiritual connection to the next generation.

The practice of blessing children has deep biblical roots. When Jacob was about to die, he called his grandsons Ephraim and Manasseh to his bedside and blessed them with words that would later be spoken by every Jewish parent: "By you shall Israel invoke blessings, saying: May God make you like Ephraim and Manasseh" (Genesis 48:20). Indeed, every Friday night we bless our sons with these words. When blessing our daughters, we invoke the names of the matriarchs: "May God make you like Sarah, Rebecca, Rachel, and Leah."

Why did Jacob choose his grandsons Ephraim and Manasseh as the models for blessing, rather than his own sons? Our sages explain that Ephraim and Manasseh were the first brothers in the Torah who did not fight with each other. Unlike Cain and Abel, Isaac and Ishmael, Jacob and Esau, or Joseph and his brothers, Ephraim and Manasseh maintained peace, even when their grandfather gave the younger brother, Ephraim, precedence over the elder, Manasseh. They teach us that siblings can love and support each other without jealousy or rivalry.

Additionally, Ephraim and Manasseh were the first Israelites raised entirely in exile in Egypt, yet they maintained their faith and identity. When we bless our children to be like them, we express our hope that they too will remain strong in their values, even in challenging environments.

The actual blessing begins with parents placing their hands on their children's heads. This gesture recalls the moment when Jacob blessed Joseph's sons, as it is written: "And Israel stretched out his right hand and laid it upon Ephraim's head" (Genesis 48:14). The physical connection creates a channel for transferring love and spiritual energy from parent to child.

The second part of the blessing comes from the priestly benediction that God taught to Aaron and his sons (Numbers 6:24-26). By using these words, we connect our private family moment to the ancient blessings once pronounced in the Temple.

Each line of the priestly blessing carries profound meaning:

"May the Lord bless you and protect you" - This refers to material blessings and physical protection. We pray that our children will have their needs met and be safe from harm.

"May the Lord make His face shine upon you and be gracious to you" - This speaks to spiritual illumination and divine favor. We pray that our children will find wisdom and grace in their life's journey.

"May the Lord lift up His face to you and grant you peace" - This highest blessing is peace, *shalom*, which in Hebrew also means completeness and wholeness. We pray that our children will find inner harmony and fulfillment.

This weekly blessing creates a unique moment of connection between parent and child. Many parents use this time to whisper personal messages of love and encouragement to each child, taking time to acknowledge their unique qualities and challenges. Others add their own prayers for their children's welfare, growth, and success.

For children, this moment of receiving their parents' blessing is deeply meaningful. Even as they grow older, many adults remember the feeling of their parents' hands on their heads, the warmth of their blessing, the special attention that made them feel seen and valued. In our busy world, this ritual creates sacred space for parent-child connection that might otherwise be lost in the rush of daily life. Some children continue to receive their parents' blessing well into adulthood, maintaining this precious connection across years and distances.

Each time we bless our children on Shabbat, we form another link in the chain of tradition that stretches back to Jacob blessing Ephraim and Manasseh. We create a moment of holiness that can transform both parent and child, strengthening family bonds and transmitting our deepest values to the next generation.

This weekly ritual reminds us that our children are not really our own but rather precious souls entrusted to our care by the Creator. When we bless them, we acknowledge this sacred trust and pray for divine help in fulfilling our awesome responsibility as parents and guardians.

Blessing the Children

Sons:

Y'simcha Elohim k'Ephraim v'chi'Menashe. Y'varechecha Adonai v'yishmerecha. Ya'er Adonai panav eilecha vichuneka. Yisa Adonai panav eilecha v'yasem l'cha shalom.

English:

May God make you like Ephraim and Manasseh. May the Lord bless you and protect you. May the Lord make His face shine upon you and be gracious to you. May the Lord lift up His face to you and grant you peace.

Daughters:

Y'simeich Elohim k'Sarah, Rivka, Rachel, v'Leah. Y'varechecha Adonai v'yishmerecha. Ya'er Adonai panav eilecha vichuneka. Yisa Adonai panav eilecha v'yasem l'cha shalom.

English:

May God make you like Sarah ,Rebecca ,Rachel ,and Leah .May the Lord bless you and protect you .May the Lord make His face shine upon you and be gracious to you .May the Lord lift up His face to you and grant you peace.

Shalom Aleichem: Peace Be Upon You

As we begin our Shabbat meal, our first act is to sing *Shalom Aleichem*, Peace be Upon You, a song that welcomes the Shabbat angels into our home. This beautiful custom is based on a remarkable teaching from the Talmud:

"Two ministering angels accompany a person home from synagogue on Friday night - one good and one bad. When they arrive home and find the candles lit, the table set, and the house in proper order for Shabbat, the good angel declares, 'May it be God's will that it should be this way next Shabbat as well,' and the bad angel must respond 'Amen' against his will. But if the house is not prepared for Shabbat, the bad angel declares, 'May it be God's will that it should be this way next Shabbat as well,' and the good angel must respond 'Amen' against his will."[4]

This teaching gave rise to the custom of singing *Shalom Aleichem*,

---

4   Babylonian Talmud, Shabbat 119b

a special hymn composed in 16th-century Safed, to greet the angels who visit our homes on Friday night. Through this song, we honor the angels and invite peace into our homes, acknowledging the importance of preparing for Shabbat both physically and spiritually.

This hymn's four verses trace a complete interaction with our heavenly guests. First we greet them, then invite them in, request their blessing, and finally bid them farewell. The number four isn't arbitrary - it recalls the angels who visited Abraham on their way to rescue Lot: "And he lifted up his eyes and looked, and behold, three men stood before him" (Genesis 18:2). Our sages teach that with the *Shechina,* the Divine Presence, accompanying them, there were actually four divine messengers.

But why do we welcome angels at all? Aren't we capable of celebrating Shabbat on our own? The answer lies in understanding what angels represent in Jewish thought. The Hebrew word for angel, *malach*, literally means "messenger." Angels represent the divine messages and spiritual forces that surround us always but that we rarely perceive in our busy lives. By acknowledging their presence as we begin Shabbat, we open ourselves to greater spiritual awareness.

Moreover, we learn from Jacob's dream of angels ascending and descending a ladder that angels connect heaven and earth. Our Shabbat table itself becomes such a ladder - a place where mundane food becomes sacred sustenance, where ordinary conversation can achieve sublime meaning. The angels we welcome help us make this transformation.

Notice that the word "peace," *shalom*, appears in every verse. This isn't coincidental. The sages teach that we are given an additional soul on Shabbat - a *neshamah yeteirah*.[5] This extra measure of spiritual awareness allows us to experience a peace that transcends our weekly concerns. The angels we welcome help usher in this deeper state of consciousness.

---

5   Babylonian Talmud, Beitzah 16a

As we finish singing *Shalom Aleichem*, our Shabbat table becomes a space where heaven and earth meet. We are now ready to celebrate the woman of valor who has led the way in creating this sacred atmosphere.

Shalom Aleichem

Shalom aleichem malachei hasharet malachei Elyon mi'Melech
Malchei Ham'lachim HaKadosh Baruch Hu

Bo'achem l'shalom malachei hashalom malachei Elyon
mi'Melech Malchei Ham'lachim HaKadosh Baruch Hu

Barchuni l'shalom malachei hashalom malachei Elyon
mi'Melech Malchei Ham'lachim HaKadosh Baruch Hu

Tzeitchem l'shalom malachei hashalom malachei Elyon
mi'Melech Malchei Ham'lachim HaKadosh Baruch Hu

English:

Peace be upon you, ministering angels, messengers of the Most High, Of the Supreme King of kings, the Holy One, blessed be He.

Come in peace, messengers of peace, messengers of the Most High, Of the Supreme King of kings, the Holy One, blessed be He.

Bless me with peace, messengers of peace, messengers of the Most High, Of the Supreme King of kings, the Holy One, blessed be He.

Go in peace, messengers of peace, messengers of the Most High, Of the Supreme King of kings, the Holy One, blessed be He.

 Scan Here to Hear this Prayer:
https://www.youtube.com/watch?v=mdR6norloZ8

Eishet Chayil: Celebrating the Woman of Valor

After blessing the children and welcoming the angels, we traditionally sing *Eishet Chayil*, A Woman of Valor (Proverbs 31:10-31).[6] These verses, which King Solomon placed at the very end of the Book of Proverbs, paint a portrait of feminine strength, wisdom, and grace that operates on multiple levels of meaning.

Eishet Chayil celebrates the importance of women, particularly wives and mothers who create and maintain homes of faith. As we sing "A woman of valor who can find? Her worth is far beyond pearls," we acknowledge that the transmission of faith and values across generations depends primarily on the spiritual power of women. While this poem comes from the Book of Proverbs, its weekly recitation reminds us of what our fast-paced modern world too often forgets: the strength of family, faith, and civilization itself rests largely on the wisdom and dedication of its women.

Consider the practical descriptions in these verses: "She rises while it is still night, and provides food for her household..." "She extends her hand to the poor, and reaches out her hands to the needy..." "She opens her mouth with wisdom, and the law of kindness is on her tongue..." "She watches over the ways of her household, and does not eat the bread of idleness..."

These verses describe a woman of remarkable capability - managing a household, engaging in commerce, caring for the poor,

---

6   While these verses appear in Proverbs as general praise for a virtuous woman, the custom of reciting them on Friday night is first mentioned in the Zohar (Part II, 14a).

teaching with wisdom, and maintaining high ethical standards. Our sages teach that while men might be the primary participants in public prayer and study, it is women who create the essential foundation of a faithful life through their work in the home.[7]

This is particularly true regarding Shabbat. It is the woman who traditionally lights the Shabbat candles, bringing physical and spiritual light into the home. It is usually the woman who prepares the special Shabbat foods, sets the table, and creates the atmosphere that makes Shabbat a delight. By singing *Eishet Chayil*, we acknowledge that without these efforts, the sublime spiritual experiences of Shabbat would not be possible.

On a deeper level, our mystics teach that *Eishet Chayil* describes the relationship between God and the people of Israel. The "woman of valor" represents the collective soul of Israel, while the husband represents God. Just as the verses describe the woman's faithfulness and dedication, so too do they mirror Israel's dedication to God through the ages.

"Her husband's heart trusts in her" - Despite all historical challenges, God maintains faith in His people.

"She does him good and not harm all the days of her life" - Israel maintains its covenant with God through all circumstances.

"Strength and dignity are her clothing" - The people of Israel maintain their spiritual dignity even in exile.

"She opens her mouth with wisdom" - This refers to Bible study and teaching.

"She looks well to the ways of her household" - Israel carefully maintains its traditions and passes them to the next generation.

At the deepest level, *Eishet Chayil* describes the *Shechinah*, the Divine Presence itself, which our mystics often describe in

---

7   In Orthodox Judaism, men are traditionally the primary participants in public prayer, which must take place at specific times, and Torah study, which requires a tremendous amount of time and dedication. Women are exempt from these obligations so they can play the leading role in establishing a spiritual foundation at home and caring for the family.

feminine terms. The woman of valor who "stretches out her hands to the poor" represents God's constant care for creation. Her rising "while it is still night" symbolizes God's presence even in times of spiritual darkness.

This explains why the poem appears in the Book of Proverbs rather than in a section about family law. It's not merely about domestic life but about the deepest structures of reality - the feminine aspects of divinity that sustain and nurture creation itself.

Even in homes without a traditional family structure, singing *Eishet Chayil* remains meaningful as a recognition of the feminine forces - both human and divine - that make Shabbat possible. Some interpret it as a song to their mothers, grandmothers, or other women who have inspired them. Others focus on its mystical meanings, seeing it as a love song between humanity and God.

The final verses sum up the poem's multiple meanings beautifully: "Grace is deceptive and beauty is illusory; It is the God-fearing woman who deserves praise. Give her credit for the fruit of her labors, And let her works praise her in the gates."

Whether we understand these words as praise for the women in our lives, for the people of Israel, or for the Divine Presence itself, they remind us that true value lies not in superficial qualities but in wisdom, kindness, and dedication to a higher purpose.

As we conclude *Eishet Chayil*, we have established the human and divine context for the Shabbat meal that follows. We have honored the feminine principle in all its manifestations - personal, national, and cosmic. Now we are ready to proceed with the *Kiddush* blessing, the formal sanctification of this holy day.

Eishet Chayil: The Woman of Valor

Eishet chayil mi yimtza, v'rachok mipninim michra
Batach ba lev ba'ala, v'shalal lo yechsar

G'malathu tov v'lo ra, kol y'mei chayeha
Darsha tzemer ufishtim, vata'as b'chefetz kapeha
Hayta ka'oniyot socher, mimerchak tavi lachma
Vatakam b'od laila, vatiten teref l'veita, v'chok l'na'aroteha
Zamema sadeh vatikachehu, mipri chapeha nat'a karem
Chagra v'oz matneha, vat'ametz zro'oteha
Ta'ama ki tov sachra, lo yichbeh balayla nera
Yadeha shilcha bakishor, v'chapeha tamchu falech
Kapa parsa le'ani, v'yadeha shilcha la'evyon
Lo tira l'veita mishaleg, ki chol beita lavush shanim
Marvadim asta la, shesh va'argaman l'vusha
Noda bash'arim ba'ala, b'shivto im ziknei aretz
Sadin asta vatimkor, vachagor natna lak'na'ani
Oz v'hadar l'vusha, vatischak l'yom acharon
Piha patcha v'chochma, v'torat chesed al l'shona
Tzofiya halichot beita, v'lechem atzlut lo tochel
Kamu vaneha vay'ashruha, ba'ala vay'hal'la
Rabot banot asu chayil, v'at alit al kulana
Sheker hachen v'hevel hayofi, isha yirat Hashem hi tithallal
T'nu la mipri yadeha, vihal'luha bash'arim ma'aseha

English:

A woman of valor who can find? Her worth is far beyond pearls

Her husband's heart trusts in her, and he lacks no fortune

She does him good and not harm, all the days of her life

She seeks wool and flax, and works with willing hands

She is like merchant ships, bringing her food from afar

She rises while it is still night and provides food for her household, and portions for her maidens

She considers a field and buys it; from her earnings she plants a vineyard

She girds her loins with strength, and makes her arms strong

She perceives that her merchandise is profitable; her lamp does not go out at night

She stretches out her hands to the distaff, and her hands grasp the spindle

She extends her hands to the poor, and reaches out her hands to the needy

She fears not for her household because of snow, for all her household is clothed in scarlet

She makes covers for herself; her clothing is fine linen and purple

Her husband is known in the gates, when he sits among the elders of the land

She makes linen garments and sells them, and supplies sashes to the merchants

Strength and dignity are her clothing, and she smiles at the future

She opens her mouth with wisdom, and loving instruction is on her tongue

She watches over the ways of her household, and does not eat the bread of idleness

Her children rise up and call her blessed; her husband also praises her

Many women have done worthily, but you surpass them all

Grace is deceitful and beauty is vain, but a woman who fears the Lord shall be praised

Give her of the fruit of her hands, and let her works praise her in the gates

---

 Scan Here to Hear this Prayer:
https://www.youtube.com/watch?v=F26T5QNtaRc

Kiddush: Sanctifying the Day

At the heart of the Friday night meal stands a ritual that directly fulfills the biblical command to "Remember the Shabbat day to keep it holy" (Exodus 20:8). This is *Kiddush*, which literally means "sanctification," when we formally declare the holiness of Shabbat over a cup of wine.

In Jewish tradition, wine symbolizes joy and celebration. The Psalmist tells us that "wine gladdens the human heart" (Psalm 104:15). By choosing wine as the medium for sanctification, we emphasize that Shabbat is not a burden but a delight. The cup used for *Kiddush* is often a family's most beautiful piece of silver or crystal, reflecting the verse "This is my God and I will beautify Him" (Exodus 15:2).

Every phrase in *Kiddush* is significant. When we say that Shabbat is "first among the holy festivals," we acknowledge that Shabbat predates all other sacred times. Unlike holidays that commemorate historical events, Shabbat was woven into the very fabric of creation.

The dual themes of Creation and Exodus found in the *Kiddush* teach us that Shabbat has both universal and particular significance. As a memorial to Creation, it speaks to all humanity about God's sovereignty and our need for sacred rest. As a reminder of the Exodus, it speaks about the freedom and spiritual liberation of the people of Israel.

The one reciting *Kiddush* traditionally stands, holding the cup in their right hand. Some have the custom to focus their eyes on the candles whose light reflects in the wine. The others at the table answer "Amen" to each blessing, making *Kiddush* a communal act of sanctification.

After the blessings, everyone at the table drinks from the *Kiddush* wine. The simple act of sharing wine from a common cup creates a powerful sense of unity among family and guests.

The recitation of *Kiddush* marks the formal beginning of the Shabbat meal. Through this ancient ritual, our dining room table is transformed into a sacred altar, our family meal into a holy feast. The sages teach that when we recite *Kiddush*, we become partners with God in proclaiming the sanctity of Shabbat.

In a world where time often feels like our enemy - always running short, always pressing us to do more, be more, achieve more - *Kiddush* gives us permission to stop. For the next twenty-five hours, we declare that we are stepping out of ordinary time into sacred time. The wine of *Kiddush* becomes our symbol of freedom from the tyranny of time, our weekly taste of eternity.

The Friday Night *Kiddush*

Yom hashishi. Vay'chulu hashamayim v'ha'aretz v'chol tz'va'am. Vay'chal Elohim bayom hashvi'i m'lachto asher asa. Vayishbot bayom hashvi'i mikol m'lachto asher asa. Vay'varech Elohim et yom hashvi'i vay'kadeish oto, ki vo shavat mikol m'lachto asher bara Elohim la'asot.

Baruch ata Adonai, Eloheinu melech ha'olam, borei p'ri hagafen.

Baruch ata Adonai, Eloheinu melech ha'olam, asher kid'shanu b'mitzvotav v'ratza vanu, v'shabbat kodsho b'ahava uv'ratzon hinchilanu, zikaron l'ma'asei v'reishit. Ki hu yom t'chila l'mikra'ei kodesh, zecher litzi'at mitzrayim. Ki vanu vacharta v'otanu kidashta mikol ha'amim, v'shabbat kodsh'cha b'ahava uv'ratzon hinchaltanu.

Baruch ata Adonai, m'kadeish hashabbat.

English:

The sixth day. And the heavens and the earth and all their hosts were completed. And God completed on the seventh day His work which He had done, and He rested on the seventh day from all His work which He had done. And God blessed the seventh day and sanctified it, for on it He rested from all His work which God created to do.

Blessed are You, Lord our God, King of the universe, who creates the fruit of the vine.

Blessed are You, Lord our God, King of the universe, who has sanctified us with His commandments and has been pleased with us, and His holy Shabbat with love and favor He has given us as a heritage, a remembrance of the Creation. For it is the first among the holy festivals, commemorating the Exodus from Egypt. For You have chosen us and sanctified us from all peoples, and Your holy Shabbat with love and favor You have given us as a heritage.

Blessed are You, Lord, who sanctifies the Shabbat.

The Hand Washing Ritual: Preparing for Sacred Eating

After *Kiddush*, but before breaking bread, Jewish tradition prescribes a ritual washing of hands. While this might seem at first glance like a simple act of hygiene, it represents something far deeper - a practice that connects us to biblical concepts of holiness and preparation before sacred service.

The Bible describes in detail how the priests would wash their hands and feet before performing sacred service: "Aaron and his sons shall wash their hands and feet from it. When they go into the Tent of Meeting, they shall wash with water, that they die not; or when they come near to the altar to minister, to cause an offering made by fire to smoke unto the Lord" (Exodus 30:19-20).

Similarly, King David proclaimed, "I will wash my hands in innocence, and I will go around Your altar, O Lord" (Psalms 26:6). These verses establish a clear biblical connection between washing hands and approaching holy service.

After the Temple's destruction, the Jewish sages sought ways to maintain this consciousness of holiness in everyday life. As we mentioned, every Jewish home is a small sanctuary, and every table set for a sacred meal is like the Temple's altar. We wash our hands before eating bread as a reminder of the priests' obligation to wash their hands in Temple times before partaking of tithes.

The washing is done with a special two-handled cup. We fill it with water, then pour twice over the right hand and twice over the left. This isn't about cleanliness - our hands should already be physically clean. Rather, this is about spiritual preparation.

After washing, we maintain silence until after eating the bread. This silence creates a space of contemplation, helping us transition from the busy chatter of life to a more elevated consciousness. It reminds us that sometimes the deepest spiritual moments require no words at all.

Consider how different our relationship with food might be if we always paused for a moment of sacred preparation before eating. In our rushed world, we often eat mindlessly, barely tasting our food, often working while we eat. This ritual teaches us to pause, to create a boundary between our mundane activities and the sacred act of eating. The water flowing over our hands can be seen as washing away distractions, helping us become fully present to the miracle of sustenance.

The prophet Isaiah described water as a symbol of divine blessing: "For I will pour water upon the thirsty land, and streams upon the dry ground; I will pour My spirit upon thy seed, and My blessing upon thine offspring" (Isaiah 44:3). Through the simple act of washing our hands before a meal, we create a moment of connection with the Divine.

Hamotzi: The Sacred Act of Breaking Bread

After the hand-washing ritual, we arrive at one of Shabbat's most iconic moments: the blessing and breaking of the *challah* bread. This ceremony is rich with biblical symbolism and historical meaning, connecting us to both the story of Creation and the miracle of the manna in the desert.

On every Shabbat table sit two whole loaves of *challah* bread, covered with a special cloth. This practice comes directly from the Torah's account of the manna: "On the sixth day they gathered twice as much bread, two *omers* for each person" (Exodus 16:22). God provided a double portion of manna on Friday so the Israelites would not need to gather food on Shabbat. Our two loaves memorialize this miracle, reminding us that God provides for those who honor the Shabbat.

The covering of the *challah* also has its source in the manna story. The Bible tells us that the manna appeared each morning with "a layer of dew before it" and "a layer of dew after it" (Exodus 16:13-14).[8] Similarly, we place our *challah* between two coverings—the tablecloth beneath and the *challah* cover above. This reminds us that even our food comes wrapped in God's love and protection.

The words of the blessing recited over bread come from Psalm 104, where King David praises God as the one "who brings forth bread from the earth" (Psalm 104:14). While it might seem obvious that bread comes from the earth, this blessing reminds us of the miraculous nature of this process: seeds decompose in the ground only to sprout new life, stalks of wheat grow from tiny kernels, and human ingenuity transforms raw grain into bread. Each step reveals divine wisdom embedded in creation.

After the blessing, the leader cuts or breaks the *challah*. Before distributing the bread, it is the custom to sprinkle or dip it in salt. This practice recalls God's words: "With all your offerings you shall offer salt" (Leviticus 2:13).[9] Since our table is compared to an altar and our meal to an offering, we include salt just as it was used in the Temple service.

The Hebrew word for bread, *lechem*, shares its root with *milchama*, the Hebrew word for "struggle" or war." This teaches us

---

8   The Mechilta d'Rabbi Ishmael, Beshalach, uses these verses as the basis for the custom of covering the challah.
9   The custom of dipping bread in salt is discussed in the Babylonian Talmud, Berachot 40a, linking the table to the Temple altar.

that bread represents humanity's constant struggle to transform and elevate the physical world. Through agriculture, milling, and baking, we partner with God in completing creation. Yet on Shabbat, we pause this struggle. The dual loaves remind us that God provides even when we cease our labors.

The braided shape of traditional *challah* hints at this interweaving of human effort and divine blessing. While the exact number of strands in a loaf of *challah* varies, six strands are common, symbolizing the six days of creation which are crowned by the Shabbat.

This sacred moment of blessing bread reminds us that even our most basic physical needs can become occasions for recognizing divine providence. By pausing before we consume bread to acknowledge its Source, we elevate the mundane act of eating to a holy act.

The Blessing Over Bread

The leader of the meal raises both loaves and recites the blessing:

Baruch ata Adonai, Eloheinu melech ha'olam, hamotzi lechem min ha'aretz.

English:

Blessed are You, Lord our God, King of the universe, who brings forth bread from the earth.

The Festive Meal: A Sacred Feast

After blessing the *challah*, we begin what the prophet calls *oneg Shabbat* - the delight of Shabbat (Isaiah 58:13). As King Solomon wrote, "Go, eat your bread with joy, and drink your wine with a glad heart, for God has already approved your works" (Ecclesiastes 9:7).

Though we fulfill the Bible's command to "remember the Shabbat day to keep it holy" (Exodus 20:8) through the *Kiddush* prayer, we also fulfill the spirit of this command through special foods and customs at our meals. This elevation of physical eating into sacred celebration follows the biblical pattern established at the Temple in Jerusalem, where festive offerings were accompanied by meat, wine, and bread (Numbers 15:3-10).

Traditional Shabbat meals often begin with fish, recalling God's blessing of creation: "Be fruitful and multiply, and fill the waters" (Genesis 1:22). Fish also symbolize God's constant providence - just as fish live suspended in water, we live constantly sustained by God's care.

The main course typically includes meat or chicken, as these foods are traditionally associated with festive meals and are enjoyed by most people, in keeping with the prophet's call to "call the Shabbat a delight" (Isaiah 58:13). However, there is no obligation to eat meat or drink wine on Shabbat. Rather, since these foods are assumed to bring joy to many, they are customarily included according to one's means. Those who do not eat meat still fulfill the obligation of Shabbat delight by preparing dishes they find especially enjoyable.

A Shabbat meal is distinguished not only by its food but also by its atmosphere. The Talmud teaches that when three people eat together and share words of Torah, it is as if they have eaten at God's table.

Traditional topics include the weekly Torah portion, ethical teachings, and stories of our sages. Many families make a practice of having each person share something they learned during the week. Others discuss how the week's Torah portion applies to contemporary life. The goal is to fulfill the biblical command to "speak of them when you sit in your house" (Deuteronomy 6:7).

Unlike hurried weekday meals, the Shabbat feast is meant

to be lingered over. Family and guests sit together, free from the distractions of phones and devices, creating a space for real conversation and connection. This fulfills the biblical ideal of family unity: "Behold, how good and how pleasant it is for brethren to dwell together in unity!" (Psalm 133:1).

Children are an integral part of the experience. Many parents use this time to really listen to their children's thoughts and experiences. The relaxed atmosphere allows for questions, stories, and the natural transmission of values across generations, fulfilling the command to "teach them diligently to your children" (Deuteronomy 6:7).

Hospitality has been a Jewish value since Abraham set the example by welcoming three strangers to his tent (Genesis 18). On Shabbat, this takes on special significance. Many families make a point of inviting guests - whether travelers, neighbors or those who might be alone.

The practice of hosting guests elevates the meal from a private family dinner to a celebration of community. When we welcome others to our table, we create what our sages call "a taste of the World to Come" - a world of peace, unity, and shared joy.

The sages teach that Shabbat is "one-sixtieth of the World to Come." Nowhere is this more evident than at the Shabbat table, where physical food becomes a vehicle for spiritual experience, where family bonds are strengthened, where strangers become friends, and where ordinary time is transformed into sacred time.

Zemirot: Songs of the Sacred Feast

It is our custom to sing with joy during the Shabbat meal. This practice fulfills King David's call to "Sing unto the Lord a new song" (Psalm 96:1) and brings to life the prophet Isaiah's vision of sacred joy: "You shall have a song as in the night when a holy feast is kept" (Isaiah 30:29).

Zemirot, the special songs sung on Shabbat, are not mere entertainment but a form of prayer and Bible study set to melody. Just as the Levites would sing in the Temple during the offerings, we elevate our meal through song. These melodies, passed down through generations, transform our dining room tables into sacred spaces where, as the Psalmist says, "My mouth shall sing praise with joyful lips" (Psalm 63:6).

The melodies of *zemirot* create an atmosphere where time seems to slow down. Many families have their own traditional tunes passed down through generations. Others incorporate new melodies, fulfilling the verse "Sing unto Him a new song" (Psalm 33:3).

Some songs focus on Shabbat's themes of creation and rest. Others speak of yearning for redemption or express love for the Bible and the commandments. Still others praise the Shabbat foods and customs themselves. Together, these melodies transform the meal beyond mere eating into a spiritual experience.

Even those who don't understand Hebrew can participate in *zemirot* through wordless melodies called *niggunim*. These tunes, often consisting of simple syllables like "lai-lai-lai" or "yai-dai-dai," can express feelings beyond words. As King David wrote, "All my bones shall say: Lord, who is like unto You?" (Psalms 35:10).

The custom of singing *zemirot* reminds us that joy isn't just an emotion but a spiritual practice. Through song, we fulfill Isaiah's prophecy that "you shall go out with joy and be led forth with peace; the mountains and the hills shall break forth before you into singing" (Isaiah 55:12).

Rabbi Nachman of Breslov captured this transformative power of Shabbat song when he taught that in the simple act of singing Shabbat songs, we discover the deepest expression of our Jewish souls. When we let go of our self-consciousness and allow ourselves to sing freely at the Shabbat table, we experience the divine presence directly, beyond what words or concepts can convey. This teaching reminds us that *zemirot* aren't about musical talent or even understanding every word - they're about opening our hearts through pure, unrestrained joy.

Yah Ribbon Olam (Lord, Master of the Universe)

This powerful Aramaic hymn, composed by 17th century Rabbi Israel Najara, expresses awe at divine creation:

Yah ribon alam v'al'maya
ant hu malka melekh malkhaya.
Ovad g'vur'teikh v'timhaya
sh'far kodamakh l'hakhavaya.

Yah ribon alam v'al'maya
ant hu malka melekh malkhaya.

Sh'vakhin asadeir tsafra v'ramsha
lakh elaha kadisha di v'ra kol nafsha,
irin kadishin uv'nei enasha,
kheivat bara, v'ofei sh'maya.

Yah ribon alam v'al'maya
ant hu malka melekh malkhaya.

Ravr'vin ov'deikh v'takifin,
makhikh r'maya v'zakif k'fifin.
Lu yikhyeh g'var sh'nin alfin
la yei'ol g'vur'teikh b'khushb'naya.

Yah ribon alam v'al'maya
ant hu malka melekh malkhaya.

Elaha di leih y'kar ur'vuta,
p'rok yat anakh mipum aryavata.
V'apeik yat amakh migo galuta,
ameikh di v'hart mikol umaya.

Yah ribon alam v'al'maya
ant hu malka melekh malkhaya.

L'mikd'sheikh tuv ul'kodesh kudshin,
atar di veih yekhedun ruhin v'nafshin.
Vizam'run lakh shirin v'rakhashin,
birush'leim karta d'shufraya.

Yah ribon alam v'al'maya
ant hu malka melekh malkhaya.

English:

God, Master of all worlds You are the King, the King of kings
The works of Your power and wonders
It is beautiful before me to declare them
You were before [all things] and You will remain [after all things]
And [in all] worlds Your presence does not depart
You are precious and You burn [with love for us]
And to You is revealed every secret and deep thing
By Your will they were created
All creatures above and below
You are King and King of kings
And ruler over all who rule
Praise, glory and greatness be

To Your precious holy Name
And the hosts of the kingdom of heaven
And on earth, from You shall be sanctified
May it be Your will that You rest
Upon me and upon Your people Israel forever
And the salvation of Your right hand show to Your people
In Your holy Temple within Your palace
And to pray, Your beloved in Your shadow
And to have mercy, Your mercy upon Your people
And may You see Zion in the building of Your palace
And gladden Your people in the service of Your altar
May it be [Your] will to accept their prayers
And all their requests at every time and season
Blessed is God Most High who created
All souls and all spirits

 Scan Here to Hear this Song:
https://www.youtube.com/watch?v=L16bkB7BDYQ

Menucha V'Simcha (Rest & Joy)

Also composed by Rabbi Najara, the themes of this song include the joy of Shabbat, God's creation, and the messianic hope. The reference to "double bread" relates to the two *challot* used on Shabbat, commemorating the double portion of manna that fell in the desert before Shabbat.

M'nukha v'simkha, or lay'hudim,
Yom shabbaton yom makhamadim.
Shom'rav v'zokh'rav heima m'idim
Ki l'shisha kol b'ru'im v'om'dim.

Sh'mei shamayim, erets v'yamim,

Kol ts'va marom g'vohim v'ramim,
Tanin v'adam v'khayat r'eimim,
Ki v'yah adonai tsur olamim.

Hu asher diber l'am s'gulato,
Shamor l'kad'sho mibo'o v'ad tseito.
Shabbat kodesh, yom khemdato,
Ki vo shavat mikol m'lakhto.

B'mitsvat shabbat eil yakhalitsakh.
Kum k'ra eilav yakhish l'am'tsakh
Nishmat kol khai v'gam na'aritsakh,
Ekhol b'simha ki kh'var ratsakh.

B'mishneh lekhem v'kiddush raba,
B'rov mat'amim v'ruakh n'diva,
Yizku l'rav tuv hamit'an'gim bah
B'viat go'eil l'hayei ha'olam haba.

English:

Rest and joy, a light for the Jews
A day of Shabbat, a day of delights
Those who guard it and remember it testify
That in six days all was created and stands
The heavens of heavens, earth and seas
All the host on high, lofty and elevated
Sea monsters and man and wild beasts
For in Yah, the Lord is the Rock of Ages
He who spoke to His treasured nation
To guard and sanctify it from its coming to its departure
The holy Shabbat, His precious day
For on it God rested from all His work

Through the commandment of Shabbat, God will strengthen you
Rise, call to Him, He will hasten to give you strength
The soul of all living things will also revere You
Eat with joy for He has already favored you
With double bread and great Kiddush
With many delicacies and a generous spirit
Those who delight in it will merit great goodness
With the coming of the Redeemer to eternal life in the World
to Come

 Scan Here to Hear this Song:
https://www.youtube.com/watch?v=sbt1-R1MaPk

Birkat Hamazon: Grace After Meals

As the Shabbat meal draws to a close, we arrive at a moment of gratitude: The Grace After Meals. The Bible commands: "And you shall eat and be satisfied, and bless the Lord your God for the good land which He has given you" (Deuteronomy 8:10).[10] Notice the precise sequence in this verse: first we eat, then we are satisfied, and only then do we bless. This ordering is deliberate and meaningful. While many spiritual traditions teach the importance of blessing food before eating, the Bible specifically commands us to express gratitude after we are satisfied.

This timing carries deep wisdom. When we are hungry and see food before us, gratitude comes naturally. But once we are satisfied, we might forget the Source of our blessing. The Bible therefore commands us to thank God precisely at the moment when we might be most likely to forget Him – when we are full and content.

---

10 This verse is the biblical source for reciting *Birkat Hamazon* (Grace After Meals). The Talmud (Berachot 48b) attributes the first blessing to Moses, the second to Joshua, the third to David and Solomon, and the fourth to the Rabbis of Yavneh.

Moses warned about this very spiritual danger: "Take heed lest... you eat and are satisfied... and your heart be lifted up, and you forget the Lord your God" (Deuteronomy 8:11-14). The practice of blessing after meals guards against this natural human tendency toward ingratitude in times of plenty.

The Grace After Meals consists of four main blessings, each focusing on a different aspect of divine kindness. The first blessing, composed by Moses himself when the manna fell in the desert, thanks God for providing food for all creatures. As the Psalmist writes, "He gives food to all flesh, for His kindness endures forever" (Psalm 136:25).

The second blessing focuses on the many gifts God has given the people of Israel - the Land of Israel, the covenant, and the Bible. This blessing fulfills the specific language of the biblical command to thank God "for the good land which He has given you."

The third blessing turns our hearts toward Jerusalem and our hopes for its restoration. This blessing reminds us that even our physical sustenance should lead us to yearn for spiritual restoration.

The fourth blessing expresses gratitude for God's constant kindness throughout history, reflecting the verse "I will sing of the kindnesses of the Lord forever" (Psalm 89:2). We acknowledge that every meal we eat is part of God's ongoing care for His creation.

On Shabbat, we add a special paragraph that weaves together our physical satisfaction from the meal with the spiritual satisfaction of Shabbat rest: "May it please You, our God, to strengthen us through Your commandments, and through the commandment of the Seventh Day, this great and holy Shabbat. For this day is great and holy before You, to refrain from work and rest thereon with love, according to the commandment of Your will..." This addition helps us fulfill Isaiah's vision of calling "the Shabbat a delight" (Isaiah 58:13), linking our enjoyment of food with our enjoyment of sacred time.

Those of us who live in wealthy countries often take our food for granted. Every meal appears through a complex system of agriculture, transportation, and commerce that obscures its ultimate Source. The practice of formally expressing gratitude after eating realigns our consciousness, reminding us that behind all human effort lies divine providence.

The Psalmist declares, "I will lift up the cup of salvation and call upon the name of the Lord" (Psalm 116:13). Through the Grace After Meals, we transform our dining table into an altar of thanksgiving, our meal into an offering of gratitude, and our satisfaction into spiritual awareness.

As we conclude our Shabbat meal with these blessings, we fulfill King David's ideal: "I will bless the Lord at all times; His praise shall continually be in my mouth" (Psalm 34:2). We have elevated our physical meal into a spiritual experience, our individual satisfaction into communal gratitude, and our table into a place of sacred awareness.

Birkat Hamazon: Grace After Meals

On Shabbat, the Grace after Meals begins with Psalm 126:

Shir hamaalot b'shuv Adonai et shivat Tzion hayinu k'cholmim. Az yimalei s'chok pinu ul'shoneinu rina, Az yomru vagoyim higdil Adonai laasot im eileh. Higdil Adonai laasot imanu hayinu s'meichim. Shuva Adonai et sh'viteinu ka'afikim banegev. Hazorim b'dimah b'rinah yiktzoru. Haloch yeileich uvacho nosei meshech hazara, Bo yavo v'rinah nosei alumotav.

A song of ascents. When the Lord will return the exiles of Zion, we will have been like dreamers. Then our mouth will be filled with laughter, and our tongue with songs of joy; then will they say among the nations, "The Lord has done great things for these." The Lord has done great things for us; we were joyful. L-rd, return our exiles as streams to arid soil. Those who sow in tears will reap with songs of joy. He goes along weeping, carrying the bag of seed; he will surely return with songs of joy, carrying his sheaves.

The Grace After Meals continues:

First Blessing:

Baruch atah Adonai Eloheinu melech ha'olam, hazan et ha'olam kulo b'tuvo b'chen b'chesed uv'rachamim. Hu noten lechem l'chol basar ki l'olam chasdo. Uv'tuvo hagadol tamid lo chasar lanu v'al yechsar lanu mazon l'olam va'ed. Ba'avur sh'mo hagadol ki hu El zan um'farnes lakol umeitiv lakol umechin mazon l'chol-b'riyotav asher bara. Baruch atah Adonai hazan et hakol.

Sacred are You, Eternal One our God, Sovereign of the cosmos, Who, with boundless goodness, sustains the entire world with grace, kindness, and compassion. You provide nourishment to all living beings, for Your loving-kindness endures forever. Through Your abundant mercy towards us continuously we do not want for food, and may we never lack sustenance, for the sake of Your mighty Name. For You, benevolent God, nourish and sustain all, bring goodness to all, and prepare sustenance for all Your creatures whom You have fashioned, as it is written: You extend Your hand and fulfill the desire of all life. Sacred are You, Eternal One, Who sustains all.

Second Blessing:

Nodeh l'cha Adonai Eloheinu al shehinchalta la'avoteinu eretz

*chemdah tovah ur'chavah, v'al shehotzeitanu Adonai Eloheinu
meï'eretz Mitzrayim uf'ditanu mibeit avadim, v'al brit'cha
shechatamta bivsareinu, v'al Torat'cha shelimadtanu, v'al chukecha
shehodatanu, v'al chayyim chen vachesed shechonantanu, v'al
achilat mazon sha'atah zan um'farnes otanu tamid, b'chol yom
uv'chol eit uv'chol sha'ah.*

*V'al hakol Adonai Eloheinu anachnu modim lach um'varchim
otach, yitbarach shimcha b'fi kol chai tamid l'olam va'ed. Kakatuv:
v'achalta v'savata uveirachta et Adonai Elohecha al ha'aretz hatovah
asher natan lach. Baruch atah Adonai al ha'aretz v'al hamazon.*

We give thanks to You, Eternal One our God, for bestowing
upon our ancestors a precious, bountiful and spacious land; for
liberating us, Eternal One our God, from the land of Egypt, and
freeing us from the house of slavery; for Your covenant which
You have sealed within us; for Your teachings which You have
shared with us; for Your laws which You have revealed to us; for
the life, grace, and kindness which You have lovingly granted us;
and for the nourishment with which You constantly sustain us
every day, at all times, and at every moment.

For all these things, Eternal One our God, we thank You and
praise You. May Your Name be blessed by every living being,
always and forever, as it is written: When you have eaten and
are fulfilled, you shall bless the Eternal One your God for the
good land which has been given to you. Sacred are You, Eternal
One, for the land and for the nourishment.

Third Blessing:

*Rachem na Adonai Eloheinu al Yisrael amecha, v'al Yerushalayim
irecha, v'al Tzion mishkan k'vodecha, v'al malchut beit David*

m'shichecha, v'al habayit hagadol v'hakadosh shenikra shimcha alav. Eloheinu avinu, r'einu, zuneinu, parn'seinu v'chalk'lenu v'harvicheinu, v'harvach lanu Adonai Eloheinu m'heira mikol tzaroteinu. V'na al tatzricheinu Adonai Eloheinu, lo lidei matnat basar vadam v'lo lidei halva'atam, ki im l'yadcha ham'lei'ah hap'tuchah hak'doshah v'har'chavah, shelo neivosh v'lo nikalem l'olam va'ed.

R'tzei v'hachalitzeinu Adonai Eloheinu b'mitzvotecha uv'mitzvat yom hash'vi'i haShabbat hagadol v'hakadosh hazeh. Ki yom zeh gadol v'kadosh hu l'fanecha lishbat bo v'lanuach bo b'ahavah k'mitzvat r'tzonecha. Uvirtzoncha haniach lanu Adonai Eloheinu shelo t'hei tzarah v'yagon va'anacha b'yom m'nuchateinu. V'har'einu Adonai Eloheinu b'nechamat Tzion irecha uv'vinyan Yerushalayim ir kodshecha ki atah hu ba'al hay'shu'ot uva'al hanechamot.

Uv'nei Yerushalayim ir hakodesh bimheirah v'yameinu. Baruch atah Adonai, boneh v'rachamav Yerushalayim. Amen.

Show compassion, Eternal One our God, upon Israel Your people, upon Jerusalem Your city, upon Zion the dwelling of Your glory, upon the kingdom of the house of David Your anointed, and upon the great and holy House which bears Your Name. Our God, our Parent, our Guardian, tend to us, sustain us, support us, and grant us abundance; and swiftly, Eternal One our God, bring relief from all our troubles. Please, Eternal One our God, do not make us reliant upon mortal gifts or loans, but rather upon Your full, open, sacred, and generous hand, that we may never know shame or disgrace.

May it be Your will, Eternal One our God, to strengthen us through Your commandments, and through the commandment of the Seventh Day, this great and holy Shabbat. For this day is great and holy before You, to cease from work and to rest thereon with love, according to Your will's command. In Your favor, Eternal One our God, grant us serenity, that there be no hardship, sorrow, or grief on our day of rest. Eternal One our God, let us witness the comfort of Zion Your city, and the restoration of Jerusalem Your holy city, for You are the Source of salvation and comfort.

Please restore Jerusalem, the holy city speedily in our time. Sacred are You, Eternal One, Who in mercy restores Jerusalem. Amen.

Fourth Blessing:

Baruch atah Adonai Eloheinu melech ha'olam, ha'El avinu malkeinu adireinu bor'einu go'aleinu yotzreinu k'dosheinu k'dosh Ya'akov, ro'einu ro'eh Yisrael, hamelech hatov v'hameitiv lakol, sheb'chol yom vayom hu heitiv, hu meitiv, hu yeitiv lanu. Hu g'malanu hu gomleinu hu yigm'leinu la'ad, l'chen ul'chesed ul'rachamim ul'revach hatzalah v'hatzlachah, b'rachah vishu'ah, nechamah parnasah v'chalkalah v'rachamim v'chayyim v'shalom v'chol tov; umikol tuv l'olam al y'chasreinu.

Sacred are You, Eternal One our God, Sovereign of the cosmos, benevolent God, our Parent, our Sovereign, our Might, our Creator, our Redeemer, our Maker, our Holy One, the Holy One of Jacob, our Guardian, the Guardian of Israel, the Sovereign who brings goodness to all, each and every day. You have done good for us, You do good for us, and You will do good for us; You have granted, You grant, and You will forever grant us grace, kindness, and mercy; solace, deliverance and prosperity; blessing and salvation; consolation, sustenance and support; compassion, life, peace, and all good things; and may we never lack any good.

Customary Additions:

Harachaman hu yimloch aleinu l'olam va'ed. Harachaman hu yitbarach bashamayim uva'aretz. Harachaman hu yishtabach l'dor dorim, v'yitpa'ar banu la'ad ul'neitzach n'tzachim, v'yit'hadar banu la'ad ul'olmei olamim. Harachaman hu y'farn'seinu b'chavod. Harachaman hu yishbor uleinu me'al tzavareinu, v'hu yolicheinu kom'miyut l'artzeinu. Harachaman hu yishlach lanu b'rachah m'rubah babayit hazeh, v'al shulchan zeh she'achalnu alav. Harachaman hu yishlach lanu et Eliyahu hanavi zachur latov, vivaser lanu b'sorot tovot y'shu'ot v'nechamot.

Harachaman hu yevarech et(avi mori) ba'al habbayit hazzeh, ve'et(immi morati) ba'alat habbayit hazzeh, otam ve'et-beitam ve'et-zar'am ve'et-kol-asher lahem otanu ve'et-kol-asher lanu, kemo shennitbarechu avoteinu, avraham yitzchak veya'akov: bakkol, mikkol, kol, ken yevarech otanu kullanu yachad, bivrachah shelemah, venomar amen:

Bamarom y'lamdu aleihem v'aleinu z'chut shet'hei l'mishmeret shalom. V'nisa v'rachah me'et Adonai, utz'dakah me'Elohei yisheinu, v'nimtza chen v'sechel tov b'einei Elohim v'adam.

Harachaman hu yanchileinu yom shekulo Shabbat um'nuchah l'chayei ha'olamim.

Harachaman hu y'zakeinu limot hamashiach ul'chayei ha'olam haba. Magdil (on special days: Migdol) y'shu'ot malko v'oseh chesed limshicho l'David ul'zar'o ad olam. Oseh shalom bimromav, hu ya'aseh shalom aleinu v'al kol Yisrael, v'imru: Amen.

Y'ru et Adonai k'doshav, ki ein machsor lirei'av. K'firim rashu v'ra'eivu, v'dorshei Adonai lo yachs'ru chol tov. Hodu l'Adonai ki

tov, ki l'olam chasdo. Pote'ach et yadecha, umasbi'a l'chol chai ratzon.
Baruch hagever asher yivtach b'Adonai, v'haya Adonai mivtacho.
Na'ar hayiti gam zakanti, v'lo ra'iti tzadik ne'ezav, v'zar'o m'vakesh
lachem. Adonai oz l'amo yiten, Adonai y'varech et amo vashalom.

May the Compassionate One reign over us for all time. May the Compassionate One be blessed in heaven and on earth. May the Compassionate One be exalted through all generations, and find glory in us forever and for all time, and be honored through us for all eternity. May the Compassionate One sustain us with dignity.

May the Compassionate One shatter our burdens, and guide us upright to our land. May the Compassionate One send abundant blessing to this house and upon this table where we have eaten. May the Compassionate One send us Elijah the prophet— may his memory be for good—who will bring tidings of joy, deliverance, and comfort. May the Compassionate One bless my father, my teacher, the master of this house, and my mother, my teacher, the mistress of this house; them, their household, their children, and all that is theirs; us, and all that is ours. As You blessed our ancestors, Abraham, Isaac and Jacob, "in all," "by all," with "all," so may You bless all of us together with a complete blessing, and let us say, Amen.

From on high, may merit be found for them and for us, bringing lasting peace. May we receive blessing from the Eternal One and kindness from the God of our salvation, and may we find grace and good understanding in the sight of God and humanity.

May the Compassionate One grant us the day that will be entirely Shabbat and rest for eternal life.

May the Compassionate One enable us to witness the days of the

Messiah and the life of the World to Come. The Eternal One is a stronghold of salvation to His sovereign, showing loving-kindness to His anointed, to David and his descendants forever. The One Who creates peace in the celestial heights, may that One create peace for us and for all Israel; and say, Amen.

Stand in awe of the Eternal One, you holy ones, for those who revere the Divine lack nothing. Young lions may grow weak and hungry, but those who seek the Eternal One shall not lack any good. Give thanks to the Eternal One for goodness, for divine kindness endures forever. You open Your hand and satisfy the will of every living thing. Blessed is the person who trusts in the Eternal One, and the Eternal One will be their protection.

CHAPTER 4

The Shabbat Morning Service - Drawing Near to God

T HE SHABBAT MORNING service is known in Hebrew as *Shacharit*, from the Hebrew word *shachar*, meaning dawn. On Shabbat morning, Jewish communities worldwide gather together to pray and praise God. Even those who find it difficult to attend synagogue services during the busy workweek make a special effort to join their communities on Shabbat morning. Through carefully preserved prayers, biblical readings, and songs passed down through generations, the service creates a powerful weekly opportunity to connect deeply with God and the people with whom we pray.

The Shabbat morning service follows a carefully designed structure that builds in spiritual intensity. Like a great symphony, it begins softly with personal prayers of gratitude, swells through psalms of praise, and builds toward several peak moments: the recitation of the *Shema*, the standing prayer called the *Amidah*, and ultimately the reading of God's Torah. Let's explore each section:

Morning Blessings: Gratitude for a New Day

The service begins with *Birchot HaShachar*, the Morning

Blessings - a series of blessings thanking God for the basic gifts of life. They remind us that every ability we have - from opening our eyes in the morning to standing upright - is a gift from God. They set the tone of gratitude that permeates the entire service.

On Shabbat, these blessings take on additional meaning. While we recite them every day, on Shabbat we have the opportunity to say them with greater focus and intentionality. The very first blessing thanks God for giving us the ability to distinguish between day and night. On Shabbat, this refers not only to physical light and darkness, but to our ability to distinguish between holy and ordinary time. The blessing for "freeing the bound" reminds us that Shabbat itself is a liberation from the constraints of the workweek.

The blessing thanking God "who straightens the bent" has a special resonance on Shabbat. During the week, we are often bent over our work, focused downward on mundane concerns. Shabbat allows us to stand upright, to lift our gaze toward heaven. Similarly, the blessing for "firming our steps" takes on new meaning - while during the week our steps may wander in many directions, on Shabbat our path is clear and directed toward spiritual matters.

The final morning blessing thanks God "who removes sleep from my eyes and slumber from my eyelids." On Shabbat, this refers not only to physical awakening but to spiritual awakening. The Prophet Isaiah criticizes those who observe Shabbat only physically while their spirits remain asleep (Isaiah 29:13). These morning blessings remind us to awaken both body and soul to the holiness of the day.

The sages teach that daily prayer was instituted to parallel the offerings in the ancient Temple.[1] Just as those offerings

---

1   This teaching appears in the Babylonian Talmud, Berachot 26b, which establishes the connection between daily prayers and Temple sacrifices.

elevated the physical into the spiritual realm, these blessings transform our mundane daily activities into opportunities for spiritual connection.

The order of the blessings follows the sequence of waking and preparing for the day. This teaches us that holiness can be found not only in obviously spiritual activities, but in the most basic functions of daily life when performed with awareness and gratitude. On Shabbat, this awareness reaches its peak as we recognize God's presence in every aspect of our existence.

Morning Blessings:

Baruch atah Adonai, Eloheinu melech ha'olam, asher natan lasechvi vinah l'havchin bein yom uvein laylah.
Blessed are You, Lord our God, King of the universe, who has given the rooster understanding to distinguish between day and night.

Baruch atah Adonai, Eloheinu melech ha'olam, she'lo asani aved.
Blessed are You, Lord our God, King of the universe, who did not make me a slave.

Baruch atah Adonai, Eloheinu melech ha'olam, poke'ach ivrim.
Blessed are You, Lord our God, King of the universe, who opens the eyes of the blind.

Baruch atah Adonai, Eloheinu melech ha'olam, matir asurim.
Blessed are You, Lord our God, King of the universe, who frees the captive.

Baruch atah Adonai, Eloheinu melech ha'olam, malbish arumim.
Blessed are You, Lord our God, King of the universe, who clothes the naked.

Baruch atah Adonai, Eloheinu melech ha'olam, zokef kefufim.
Blessed are You, Lord our God, King of the universe, who straightens the bent.

Baruch atah Adonai, Eloheinu melech ha'olam, roka ha'aretz al hamayim.
Blessed are You, Lord our God, King of the universe, who spreads the earth upon the waters.

Baruch atah Adonai, Eloheinu melech ha'olam, hameichin mitzadei gaver.
Blessed are You, Lord our God, King of the universe, who firms a person's footsteps.

Baruch atah Adonai, Eloheinu melech ha'olam, she'asah li kol tzorki.
Blessed are You, Lord our God, King of the universe, who has provided me with all my needs.

Baruch atah Adonai, Eloheinu melech ha'olam, hanoten laya'ef ko'ach.
Blessed are You, Lord our God, King of the universe, who gives strength to the weary.

Baruch atah Adonai, Eloheinu melech ha'olam, hama'avir sheina me'einai ut'numa me'afapai.
Blessed are You, Lord our God, King of the universe, who removes sleep from my eyes and slumber from my eyelids.

Verses of Song: The Pesukei D'Zimra

The next major section is called *Pesukei D'Zimra*, Verses of Song - a collection of psalms and biblical passages focusing on praise of God. This section fulfills David's words in Psalm 34:1: "I will bless the Lord at all times; His praise shall continually be in my mouth."

One of the most beautiful prayers in the Shabbat morning service is *Nishmat Kol Chai* (The Soul of Every Living Thing), which is recited only on Shabbat and festivals. This prayer reminds us that Shabbat is not just about what we don't do (refraining from work), but about forming a relationship with God. It fulfills the verse "Let everything that has breath praise the Lord" (Psalm 150:6).

The timing of this prayer is significant. We recite it at the conclusion of the Verses of Song section of the service, as a culmination of all our praises. Just as Shabbat represents the pinnacle of Creation, *Nishmat* represents the pinnacle of our prayers of praise.

The prayer begins with a striking image - not just humans, but every living soul praises God. On Shabbat, we become aware that we are part of a cosmic chorus of praise. The trees, animals, and even the angels join together in exalting their Creator. On Shabbat, all of Creation is elevated to a higher spiritual plane.

Nishmat then moves into what might be called "holy hyperbole" - even if our mouths were as full of song as the sea, and our tongues as full of joyous song as its waves, we still could not adequately thank God. This poetic passage teaches us an important lesson about gratitude. No matter how much we express our thanks, we can never fully articulate our appreciation for the gift of life itself. On Shabbat, when we step back from creating and simply exist in God's creation, this awareness becomes especially acute.

The prayer goes on to enumerate specific things for which we are grateful - liberation from Egypt, sustenance in times of famine, protection from enemies and disease. This listing of historical events is particularly appropriate for Shabbat, which the Torah describes as a remembrance of both Creation (Exodus 20:11) and the Exodus from Egypt (Deuteronomy 5:15). Through this prayer, we fulfill both aspects of Shabbat - celebrating Creation and remembering our redemption.

Another remarkable aspect of *Nishmat* is its description of bodily praise - every mouth shall thank God, every tongue shall swear allegiance, every knee shall bend. Serving God is not just a spiritual activity but involves our entire being. On Shabbat, both body and soul participate in divine service. We express this through physical pleasures like festive meals as well as spiritual activities like prayer.

The conclusion of *Nishmat* speaks of the "assemblies of the myriads of Your people, the House of Israel." This reminds us that while each individual's praise is precious, there is something especially powerful about communal prayer. Shabbat brings the people of Israel together in a unique way, and *Nishmat* captures this spirit of unified praise.

The placement of *Nishmat* at the end of the Verses of Song serves as a bridge to the next section of the service, the *Shema* and its blessings. Having expressed our gratitude and praise, we are ready to accept God's sovereignty and unite with the angels in declaring God's holiness. This progression mirrors the journey of Shabbat itself - from appreciation of Creation to intimate connection with the Creator.

Nishmat Kol Chai

Nishmat kol chai t'vareich et shimcha, Adonai Eloheinu, v'ru'ach kol basar t'fa'er ut'romem zicharcha malkeinu tamid. Min ha'olam v'ad ha'olam atah El, u'mibaladecha ein lanu melech, go'el u'moshi'a, podeh u'matzil, v'oneh um'rachem b'chol eit tzarah v'tzukah. Ein lanu melech ela atah.

The soul of every living being shall bless Your Name, Lord our God, and the spirit of all flesh shall continually glorify and exalt Your remembrance, our King. From eternity to eternity You are

God, and besides You we have no King, Redeemer, or Savior, who liberates, rescues, sustains, and shows mercy in all times of trouble and distress. We have no King but You.

Elohei harishonim v'ha'acharonim, Eloha kol briyot, Adon kol toladot, hamehulal b'rov hatishbachot, ham'naheg olamo b'chesed uv'riyotav b'rachamim. V'Adonai lo yanum v'lo yishan - ham'orer y'sheinim v'hameikitz nirdamim, v'hameisi'ach ilmim v'hamatir asurim v'hasomech noflim v'hazokef k'fufim.

God of the first and the last, God of all creatures, Master of all generations, who is extolled through a multitude of praises, who guides His world with kindness and His creatures with mercy. The Lord neither slumbers nor sleeps - He rouses the sleepers and awakens the slumberers, gives speech to the mute, releases the bound, supports the fallen and straightens the bent.

L'cha l'vadcha anachnu modim. Ilu finu malei shirah kayam, ul'shoneinu rinah kahamon galav, v'siftoteinu shevach k'merchavei rakia, v'eineinu me'irot kashemesh v'chayarei'ach, v'yadeinu prusot k'nishrei shamayim, v'ragleinu kalot ka'ayalot - ein anachnu maspikim l'hodot l'cha, Adonai Eloheinu v'Elohei avoteinu, ul'vareich et shimcha al achat mei'elef alfei alafim v'ribei r'vavot p'amim hatovot she'asita im avoteinu v'imanu.

To You alone we give thanks. If our mouths were as full of song as the sea, and our tongues as full of joyous song as its multitude of waves, and our lips as full of praise as the breadth of the heavens, and our eyes as brilliant as the sun and the moon, and our hands as outspread as eagles of the sky, and our feet as swift as deer - we still would not sufficiently thank You, Lord our God and God of our ancestors, and bless Your Name for even one of the thousand thousands and myriad myriads of favors that you performed for our ancestors and for us.

Mimitzrayim g'altanu, Adonai Eloheinu, umibeit avadim p'ditanu, b'ra'av zantanu uv'sava kilkaltanu, meicherev hitzaltanu umidever milat'tanu, umeichalayim ra'im v'ne'emanim dilitanu.

From Egypt You redeemed us, Lord our God, and from the house of bondage You liberated us. In famine You nourished us and in plenty You sustained us. From the sword You saved us, from plague You delivered us, and from severe and enduring diseases You spared us.

Ad heina azarunu rachamecha v'lo azavunu chasadecha, v'al tit'sheinu Adonai Eloheinu lanetzach. Al kein eivarim shepilagta banu v'ru'ach un'shamah shenafachta b'apeinu v'lashon asher samta b'finu - hein heim yodu vivarchu vishab'chu vifa'aru virom'mu v'ya'aritzu v'yak'dishu v'yamlichu et shimcha malkeinu.

Until now Your mercies have helped us, and Your kindnesses have not forsaken us; and do not abandon us, Lord our God, forever. Therefore, the limbs which You have arranged within us and the spirit and soul which You have breathed into our nostrils, and the tongue which You have placed in our mouth - they all shall thank, bless, praise, glorify, exalt, revere, sanctify, and declare the sovereignty of Your Name, our King.

Ki chol peh l'cha yodeh, v'chol lashon l'cha tishava, v'chol berech l'cha tichra, v'chol komah l'fanecha tishtachaveh, v'chol l'vavot yira'ucha, v'chol kerev uch'layot y'zamru lishmecha, kadavar shekatuv, kol atzmotai tomarna Adonai mi chamocha matzil ani meichazak mimenu v'ani v'evyon migozlo.

For every mouth shall give thanks to You, every tongue shall swear allegiance to You, every knee shall bend to You, every erect body shall bow before You, all hearts shall fear You, and all innermost feelings and thoughts shall sing praises to Your Name, as it is written: "All my bones shall say: O Lord, who is like You? You save the poor man from one who is stronger than he, the poor and the destitute from one who would rob him."

Mi yidmeh lach umi yishveh lach umi ya'aroch lach ha'El hagadol hagibor v'hanora El elyon konei shamayim va'aretz. N'hallelcha un'shabeichacha un'fa'ercha un'vareich et sheim kodshecha, ka'amur: L'David, barchi nafshi et Adonai v'chol k'ravai et sheim kodsho.

Who can be compared to You, who is equal to You, who can be measured against You? O great, mighty, and awesome God, supreme God, Creator of heaven and earth. We will praise You, laud You, glorify You, and bless Your holy Name, as it is said: "By David: Bless the Lord, O my soul, and let my whole inner being bless His holy Name."

Ha'El b'ta'atzumot uzecha, hagadol bichvod sh'mecha, hagibor lanetzach v'hanora b'norotecha, hamelech hayoshev al kisei ram v'nisa.

O God, in the power of Your strength, great in the glory of Your Name, mighty forever and awesome in Your awesome deeds, the King who sits upon a high and lofty throne.

Shochein ad marom v'kadosh sh'mo. V'katuv: ran'n'nu tzadikim b'Adonai, lay'sharim nava t'hilah.

He who dwells for eternity, exalted and holy is His Name. And it is written: "Sing joyfully to the Lord, you righteous; it befits the upright to offer praise."

B'fi y'sharim tit'romam, uv'divrei tzadikim titbarach, uvilshon chasidim titkadash, uv'kerev k'doshim tit'halal.

By the mouth of the upright You shall be exalted; by the words of the righteous You shall be blessed; by the tongue of the pious You shall be sanctified; and among the holy ones You shall be praised.

Uv'mak'halot riv'vot amcha beit Yisrael b'rinah yitpa'er shimcha malkeinu b'chol dor vador. Shekein chovat kol hay'tzurim l'fanecha Adonai Eloheinu veilohei avoteinu l'hodot l'halel l'shabei'ach l'fa'er l'romem l'hader l'vareich l'alei ul'kaleis al kol divrei shirot v'tishbachot David ben Yishai avd'cha m'shichecha.

And in the assemblies of the myriads of Your people, the House of Israel, Your Name shall be glorified with joyous song in every generation. For such is the duty of all creatures before You, Lord our God and God of our ancestors, to thank, to praise, to laud, to glorify, to exalt, to adore, to bless, to elevate and to honor You, even beyond all the words of songs and praises of David, the son of Jesse, Your servant, Your anointed.

The Shema: Declaring God's Unity

After the Verses of Song, we reach one of the spiritual peaks of the service - the recitation of the *Shema* and its blessings. The three paragraphs from the Bible that make up the *Shema* prayer (Deuteronomy 6:4-9, 11:13-21, and Numbers 15:37-41) form the central declaration of Jewish faith.[2]

The Amidah: Standing Before God

The climax of the service is the *Amidah* (literally "standing") prayer. At its heart is a beautiful blessing that weaves together the major themes of Shabbat - Creation, the revelation at Mount Sinai, and our weekly observance of this sacred day. The prayer reminds

---

2   See Chapter 2 for an in-depth exploration of the *Shema* and its unique resonance on Shabbat.

us that Shabbat is both a sign of God's special covenant with Israel and a testament to His creation of the world. When we recite "You sanctified the seventh day for Your name's sake, as the culmination of the creation of heaven and earth," we affirm both the universal message of Shabbat - that God created the world in six days and rested on the seventh - and its particular significance to the people of Israel as an "inheritance" and source of sanctification.

The Amidah: Shabbat Morning Blessing

Yismach Moshe bematnat chelko, ki eved ne'eman karata lo.
Kelil tif'eret b'rosho natata, be'amdo lefanekha al Har Sinai.
U'shnei luchot avanim horid b'yado, v'katavta vahem
shemirat Shabbat.
V'chen katuv b'Toratecha:

V'shamru v'nei Yisrael et haShabbat, la'asot et haShabbat
l'dorotam brit olam.
Beini u'vein b'nei Yisrael ot hi l'olam, ki sheishet yamim asah
Hashem et haShamayim v'et ha'aretz,
u'vayom ha'shevi'i shavat va'yinafash.

V'lo netato Hashem Elokeinu l'goyei ha'aratzot, v'lo hinchalto
Malkeinu l'ovdei pesilim.
V'gam b'menuchato lo yishkenu areilim, ki l'Yisrael amcha
netato b'ahava,
l'zera Yaakov asher bam bacharta. Am mekadshei shevi'i, kulam
yisbe'u v'yit'angu mituvecha.
U'va'shevi'i ratzita bo v'kiddashto, chemdat yamim oto karata,
zecher l'ma'asei bereishit.

Elokeinu v'Elohei avoteinu, retze v'menuchateinu. Kadsheinu

b'mitzvotecha, v'ten chelkeinu b'Toratecha.
Sabeinu mituvecha, u'samcheinu bi'yeshuatecha, v'taher libeinu
l'ovd'cha be'emet.
V'hanchileinu Hashem Elokeinu b'ahava u'v'ratzon Shabbat
kodshecha, v'yanuchu vo Yisrael mekadshei shemecha.

Baruch ata Adonai, mekadesh haShabbat.

English:

Moses rejoiced in the gift of his portion, for "trusted servant"
You called him.
A crown of glory You placed on his head, as he stood before
You on Mount Sinai.
And two tablets of stone he brought down in his hand, and on
them You wrote the observance of Shabbat.
And so it is written in Your Torah:

"The children of Israel shall keep the Shabbat, to make the
Shabbat an eternal covenant for their generations.
Between Me and the children of Israel it is a sign forever, for
in six days Hashem made the heavens and the earth, and on
the seventh day He ceased and rested."

You did not give it, Hashem our God, to the nations of the
lands, nor did You bequeath it to idol worshipers.
And in its rest the uncircumcised shall not dwell, for to Israel,
Your people, You gave it with love,
to the seed of Jacob, whom You chose. A nation that sanctifies
the seventh day, they all shall be satisfied and delight in
Your goodness. And on the seventh day, You favored it
and sanctified it, the most desirable of days You called it, a
remembrance of the act of Creation.

Our God and God of our ancestors, accept our rest. Sanctify us with Your commandments, and give us our portion in Your Torah. Satiate us with Your goodness, and gladden us with Your salvation. Purify our hearts to serve You in truth. And grant us, Hashem our God, lovingly and willingly, Your holy Shabbat as an inheritance, and may Israel, who sanctify Your Name, rest on it. Blessed are You, Hashem, Who sanctifies the Shabbat.

The Power of Communal Prayer

While God certainly hears individual prayer, there is a special power in communal prayer. The sages teach that God never rejects the prayers of a community, based on Job's words: "Behold, God is mighty, and does not despise any" (Job 36:5). This reflects King Solomon's words at the dedication of the First Temple, when he prayed that God would hear "the prayer and supplication of Your people Israel" (1 Kings 8:52).

The sages derived from the verse "in the multitude of people is the king's glory" (Proverbs 14:28) that the more people who gather to pray together, the more God's glory is magnified. This is why Jewish law requires a minimum of ten adult men[3] (called a *minyan*) for certain prayers to be recited - it ensures that prayer remains primarily a communal rather than individual experience. Each of us, on our own, is flawed and incomplete. But when we join together, our prayers combine to create a complete and powerful expression of devotion to God.

At first glance, we might assume that private prayer would be more heartfelt and personally meaningful, better addressing

---

3   In traditional Orthodox practice, only men are counted toward a minyan. This is based on several factors: the exemption of women from time-bound positive commandments (which includes many prayer obligations), the derivation of the requirement for ten from biblical passages where men were specifically gathered, and the interpretation of the word "congregation" (*edah*) as referring to the ten adult male spies sent to scout the land of Canaan (Numbers 14:27).

our individual circumstances and needs. Yet despite the value of these personal moments with God, the Jewish tradition teaches that our primary purpose is to sanctify God's Name and connect all aspects of creation to their spiritual source. This sacred work requires us to transcend our individuality and embrace our role within the larger community.

This communal orientation is woven throughout Jewish prayer. Notice how the weekday *Amidah* consistently uses plural language: "Heal us," "Bless this year for us," and "Gather our exiles." Even when praying silently, the Jewish worshipper speaks not just for themselves but as part of a collective voice.

What makes the Jewish people unique is their capacity to manifest holiness (*kedushah*) as a community. While righteous individuals exist among all peoples, the revelation of holiness through an entire nation is expressed uniquely through Israel. This is why Israel received the Torah collectively and why the Temple—the physical dwelling place of God's presence on earth—was built as a national sanctuary. Even in a small way, when ten Jews gather for prayer, they participate in and manifest this collective holiness.

Therefore, when we engage with Shabbat practices, we benefit greatly from embracing both individual and communal dimensions of prayer. When we join with others, identifying with their struggles and lifting up their needs alongside our own, our personal prayers become connected to something larger than ourselves.

The Weekly Bible Reading

The public reading of the Bible during the Saturday morning service is one of Judaism's most ancient and important practices. Jewish sages trace the tradition of Torah reading on Shabbat morning back to Moses' time in the desert. This practice continues unbroken to this day, ensuring that the Bible remains not just a sacred text, but a living part of community life.

The Torah scroll used for this reading is itself a work of great sanctity. It is handwritten by a skilled scribe on parchment using special ink and traditional calligraphy, exactly as Torah scrolls have been written for thousands of years. The scroll contains the text of the Five Books of Moses without vowels, punctuation, or musical notes, which must be memorized by the reader. This preservation of the ancient tradition creates a powerful link between modern Jewish communities and their biblical ancestors.

The reading begins with a dramatic ceremony. The ark, a cabinet at the front of the synagogue containing the Torah scrolls, is opened, and the congregation stands as we recite the words Moses spoke when the Ark of the Covenant would journey in the wilderness: "Arise, O Lord, and let Your enemies be scattered, and let those who hate You flee before You" (Numbers 10:35).

The Torah scroll is then carried in procession through the synagogue while the congregation sings Psalm 34:4: "Declare with me the greatness of the Lord, and let us exalt His name together." As the Torah passes, people reach out to touch it with their prayer books or prayer shawls and then kiss the book or shawl - a gesture of love for God's word that brings to mind the Psalmist's words, "O how I love Your law! It is my meditation all the day" (Psalm 119:97).

The Torah is read according to a traditional system of musical notes that has been passed down through the generations. These musical notes are not mere decorations - they serve as punctuation marks and guides for emphasis, helping to convey the meaning of the text. This fulfills what we read in Nehemiah 8:8, that the Torah should be read "distinctly...giving the sense so that the people understood the reading."

The Shabbat morning reading is divided into seven sections, plus a concluding reading. Different members of the congregation are called up for each section. This practice reflects the biblical idea that the Bible was given to all of Israel, not just to the priests or leaders. Before and after each reading, the person called up recites a blessing thanking God for giving His Torah to the people of Israel.

Through this weekly reading, the Bible becomes not just a book we respect, but a story we live. We don't just read about Abraham, Isaac, and Jacob - we relive their experiences, challenges, and triumphs. Their story becomes our story, their God our God, their mission our mission. This is what Moses meant when he said, "The Lord our God made a covenant with us at Horeb. The Lord did not make this covenant with our fathers, but with us, those who are here today, all of us who are alive" (Deuteronomy 5:2-3).

Each year in the fall, Jewish communities complete the reading of the Five Books of Moses and immediately begin again with Genesis. This annual cycle creates a rhythm to Jewish life, as regular as the seasons. Just as nature moves through its yearly cycle of spring, summer, fall, and winter, the biblical narrative cycles through our lives, becoming deeper and richer with each annual reading.

This yearly renewal reflects the inexhaustible nature of God's word. Each time we complete the cycle through the entire Five Books of Moses, we approach the familiar text at a different point in our lives, discovering new insights, relevance, and inspiration. As King David prayed, "Open my eyes, that I may see wondrous things from Your law" (Psalm 119:18). The Bible's wisdom is boundless - its waters are deep and vast, yet even a child can wade in and drink. This is why King Solomon taught that "The words of the wise are like goads" (Ecclesiastes 12:11) - they continually prod us toward growth and understanding, no matter how many times we encounter them.

The Jewish approach to reading the Bible is unique. The Five Books of Moses (Genesis through Deuteronomy) are divided into 54 portions, and each week Jewish communities worldwide read and study the same portion. But this is not merely about studying an ancient text or learning historical events. Rather, as one of Judaism's great teachers, Rabbi Schneur Zalman of Liadi (1745-1812), taught his followers: "One must live with the times."[4]

This cryptic teaching puzzled even his closest students until its meaning was explained: We must not just read the weekly portion of the Bible, but actually experience it and live it in our own lives. This transforms Bible reading from an intellectual exercise into a deeply personal spiritual journey.

Rabbi Yosef Yitzchak Schneersohn once shared an experience from his childhood in 1891: One Saturday morning, as a boy of eleven, he found his father reviewing the weekly Bible reading, which that week was from Genesis 12-17 - the section where God calls Abraham to leave his homeland. His father was simultaneously in an elevated mood yet had tears streaming down his face. Later, when the young boy gathered the courage to ask about this seeming contradiction, his father explained they were "tears of joy" and shared a profound teaching:

"The first portion of Genesis is a happy portion - God is creating the universe and is satisfied 'that it is good.' The next portion brings the flood - it's a depressing week, but ends happily with Abraham's birth. But the truly joyous week is this one, where we read about God's call to Abraham. Every day of this week, we live our lives together with Abraham - the first person to sacrifice himself to bring awareness of God to the world."

This way of reading transforms how we understand the Bible's stories. When we read about Abraham's journey from his homeland, we don't just learn about a historical event - we contemplate our own spiritual journeys and the sacrifices they require. The Exodus from Egypt becomes more than an ancient story of liberation - it prompts us to examine what enslaves us today and

---

4   Rabbi Menachem Mendel Schneerson, HaYom Yom, a collection of Chassidic teachings, 2 Cheshvan

how we might achieve greater freedom. The detailed accounts of building the Tabernacle in the wilderness inspire us to consider how we can make space for God in our own lives. When we read about the giving of the Ten Commandments at Mount Sinai, we find ourselves renewed in our own commitment to God's word.

This approach makes the Bible not just a historical document but a living, breathing guide to life. Each week's portion becomes a lens through which we view our current experiences and challenges. The verses "Your word is a lamp to my feet and a light to my path" (Psalm 119:105) take on new meaning - the Bible illuminates not just ancient history but our own lives, today.

When Jewish communities worldwide read the same portion each week, it creates a powerful spiritual unity. A businessman in New York, a soldier in Israel, and a teacher in London are all contemplating the same biblical passages, finding personal meaning in the same verses, and living with the same spiritual themes. This fulfills God's vision of Israel as "a kingdom of priests and a holy nation" (Exodus 19:6). The people of Israel are united by their engagement with His word.

In practice, this system means that the Bible becomes woven into the fabric of daily Jewish life. The weekly portion becomes a topic of discussion at family meals, the focus of study groups, and the subject of the rabbi's sermon. Children learn about it in religious schools, families discuss it at home, and individuals reflect on its lessons throughout their week.

For instance, during the week when we read about Joseph forgiving his brothers who sold him into slavery, people discuss what it means to truly forgive and how to overcome resentment toward those who have wronged us. They consider the role of family reconciliation in God's plan. When reading about the Israelites complaining in the wilderness despite God's miracles, we examine our own tendency to take blessings for granted and consider how to cultivate a more grateful attitude.

This approach makes Bible study not just an academic exercise but a transformative spiritual practice that shapes how we view and live our lives. Each story becomes not just something that happened long ago, but a source of wisdom and guidance for our present challenges and opportunities.

The Musaf Service: Remembering the Temple

After the Torah reading concludes, Jewish congregations proceed to what is called the *Musaf* service ("*musaf*," meaning "additional" in Hebrew). This unique prayer service helps us understand an important aspect of biblical worship and keeps alive the memory and hope of its restoration.

To understand the *Musaf* service, we need to look back to the Bible's description of worship in ancient times. The Book of Numbers describes how each day, the priests would offer two lambs as sacrifices in the Temple in Jerusalem. On Shabbat, they would offer an additional two lambs:

"On the Shabbat day, two male lambs in their first year, without blemish, and two-tenths of an ephah of fine flour mixed with oil as a grain offering, and its drink offering - this is the burnt offering of every Shabbat, besides the regular burnt offering and its drink offering" (Numbers 28:9-10).

When the Second Temple in Jerusalem was destroyed by the Romans in 70 CE, the Jewish people faced a profound crisis: how could they maintain their relationship with God without the Temple service that the Bible prescribed? They found guidance in the words of the prophet Hosea, who had said: "Take words with you and return to the Lord... and we will offer the sacrifices of our lips instead of bulls" (Hosea 14:3). The prophet's words imply that heartfelt prayer could take the place of physical offerings.[5]

The early sages therefore established Jewish prayers to

---

5   Babylonian Talmud, Berachot 26b.

correspond with the Temple's schedule of offerings. Just as there was an additional sacrifice on Shabbat, we have an additional prayer service - *Musaf*. In this way, the ancient pattern of worship continues through prayer, even without the physical Temple.

The *Musaf* service serves as a bridge between past and future. It helps us remember the ancient Temple service while also expressing our hope for its restoration.

The central prayer of the Musaf service expresses this dual focus: "May it be Your will, Lord our God and God of our ancestors, that You have mercy on us and speedily rebuild Your Temple in our days... Then we will be able to fulfill the obligations of Your will and perform our duties before You through the daily offerings in their proper order and the additional offerings according to their regulation..."

This prayer reminds us that while we can no longer offer physical sacrifices, our longing to serve God remains unchanged. The *Musaf* service transforms that longing into words of prayer and praise.

But *Musaf* is more than just a memorial service. It teaches several critical spiritual lessons. First, it reminds us that worship requires sacrifice. While we no longer bring animal offerings, we still must "sacrifice" our time, comfort, and distractions to focus on prayer and drawing near to God. Second, it demonstrates how ancient biblical practices can be meaningfully adapted when circumstances change. The Jewish people did not abandon worship when the Temple was destroyed; they found new ways to fulfill the Bible's deeper purpose. Third, it keeps alive the hope of restoration prophesied in Scripture. The prophets spoke of a time when "My house shall be called a house of prayer for all peoples" (Isaiah 56:7), and when "Many peoples shall come and say, 'Come, let us go up to the mountain of the Lord, to the house of the God of Jacob'" (Isaiah 2:3).

The centerpiece of the *Musaf* service is a beautiful prayer that connects the sanctity of Shabbat with the ancient Temple service. This prayer beautifully weaves together several themes: the joy of Shabbat observance, the memory of the Temple service, and the hope for restoration. It connects the weekly Shabbat to both the past (the Creation and the giving of the Bible at Sinai) and the future (the hoped-for restoration of Temple worship). Most importantly, it emphasizes that Shabbat is not a burden but a delight. Those who observe it "shall inherit eternal glory" and "merit eternal life."

While the *Musaf* service is uniquely Jewish, its underlying message speaks to all who love God. Our forms of worship may change, but our dedication to serving God remains constant. This theme of steadfast devotion resonates with the prophetic hope of universal worship in Jerusalem, as proclaimed by the prophet Zechariah: "And the Lord shall be King over all the earth. On that day there shall be one Lord, and His name one" (Zechariah 14:9).

The *Musaf* service thus completes the Shabbat morning prayers by connecting us to our biblical past while inspiring hope for humanity's future. It reminds us that while we live in the present, our worship should be informed by the past and oriented toward the future that God has promised.

The Mussaf Amidah: Shabbat Blessing

Tikanta Shabbat ratzita korbenoteha, tzivita perusheha im sidurei nesacheha. Me'angeha le'olam kavod yinchalu, to'ameha chaim zachu, ve'gam ha'ohavim devareha gedula bacharu. Az mi'sinai nitztavu aleha. Vatetzavenu Adonai Eloheinu lehakriv bah korban musaf Shabbat kara'ui.

Yehi ratzon milfanecha Adonai Eloheinu ve'Elohei avoteinu, sheta'alenu be'simcha le'artzenu, vetita'enu bigvulenu. Ve'sham na'aseh lefanecha et korbenot chovoteinu, temidim ke'sidram umusafim ke'hilchatam. Ve'et musaf yom haShabbat hazeh, na'aseh ve'nakriv lefanecha be'ahavah ke'mitzvat retzonecha. Kemo shekatavta aleinu be'toratecha al yedei Moshe avdecha mipi kevodecha ka'amur:

Uveyom haShabbat, shnei kevasim benei shana temimim, ushnei esronim solet mincha belulah vashemen ve'nisko. Olat Shabbat be'Shabbato al olat hatamid ve'niskah.

Yismechu bemalchutcha shomrei Shabbat ve'korei oneg. Am mekadshei shevi'i, kulam yisbe'u ve'yit'angu mituvecha. Uvashevi'i ratzita bo ve'kidashto, chemdat yamim oto karata, zecher lema'aseh bereishit.

Eloheinu ve'Elohei avoteinu, retzeh bimnuchateinu. Kadshenu be'mitzvotecha ve'ten chelkenu be'toratecha. Sab'enu mituvecha ve'samchenu bishuatecha. Ve'taher libenu le'ovdecha be'emet. Ve'hanchilenu Adonai Eloheinu be'ahavah uve'ratzon Shabbat kodshecha, ve'yanuchu vo Yisrael mekadshei shemecha.

Baruch atah Adonai, mekadesh haShabbat.

English:

You established the Shabbat and found favor in its offerings, prescribed its explanations along with the arrangement of its libations. Those who delight in it shall inherit eternal glory; those who taste it merit life; those who love its precepts have chosen greatness. At Sinai they were commanded concerning it. You commanded us, Lord our God, to offer on it the additional Shabbat offering appropriately.

May it be Your will, Lord our God and God of our ancestors, that You bring us up in joy to our Land and plant us within our borders. There we will perform before You our obligatory offerings - the daily offerings in their order and the additional offerings according to their laws. And this Shabbat day's additional offering we will prepare and offer before You with love, according to Your will's commandment, as You have written for us in Your Torah through Moses Your servant, from Your glorious mouth, as it is said:

"On the Shabbat day: two male lambs in their first year, unblemished, and two tenth-measures of fine flour as a meal-offering, mixed with oil, and its libation. The burnt-offering of each Shabbat on its Shabbat, in addition to the continuous burnt-offering and its libation."

Those who observe Shabbat and call it a delight shall rejoice in Your sovereignty. The people who sanctify the seventh day - they will all be satisfied and delighted from Your goodness. And the seventh day - You found favor in it and sanctified it; the most cherished of days You called it, a remembrance of the work of Creation.

Our God and God of our ancestors, may our rest be pleasing to You. Sanctify us with Your commandments and grant our portion in Your Torah. Satisfy us from Your goodness and gladden us with Your salvation. Purify our hearts to serve You in truth. And grant us as our heritage, Lord our God, with love and favor, Your holy Shabbat, and may Israel, who sanctify Your Name, rest on it.

Blessed are You, Lord, Who sanctifies the Shabbat.

CHAPTER 5

Living the Shabbat Day

I N OUR HYPER-CONNECTED world, the idea of spending twenty-five hours without phones, computers, television, or social media might sound impossible, even terrifying. Yet this "digital Shabbat" may be exactly what we need most.

The biblical command to rest on the Shabbat takes on new meaning in our age of constant connectivity. While the Bible speaks of refraining from work and commerce, today we must also grapple with the endless stream of notifications, updates, news alerts, and social media that fragment our attention and drain our spiritual energy.

Charlie Kirk, a prominent conservative activist and media figure, has embraced the practice of completely disconnecting from technology for the Shabbat with his wife. Despite—or perhaps because of—his high-profile public role and large social media following, Kirk turns off his phone every Friday evening and places it in a drawer, where it remains until the Shabbat ends on Saturday night.

"The Shabbat day is restorative," Kirk explains. "It's a gift to mankind." His wife Erika notes that in our current cultural climate, "if you don't take time to literally quiet your mind from the noise of life you will be inundated. From news articles to press releases, to your friend doing something... it's really something special to be aligned with the Shabbat, to be able to just take the time to just breathe, cut out the noise."[1]

The Kirks' experience reflects a growing recognition among people of faith that our relationship with technology needs boundaries. The constant stream of information and interaction leaves little room for quiet contemplation, deep relationships, or genuine rest. Shabbat is our weekly opportunity to break free from this digital bondage.

When God commands us to rest on Shabbat, He calls us to cease from our work (*shavat*) as He Himself did on the seventh day: "And on the seventh day God finished His work that He had done, and He rested (*vayishbot*) on the seventh day from all His work that He had done" (Genesis 2:2). While the Torah uses forms of *shavat* (to cease) for Shabbat rest, the sages drew a connection to another biblical concept: "menucha."

In Scripture, *menucha* originally referred to the promised land of Israel - "For you have not yet come to the resting place (menucha) or to the inheritance, which the Lord, your God, is giving you" (Deuteronomy 12:9). The sages recognized that just as the physical promised land offered rest from wandering, Shabbat offers a spiritual promised land in time.[2] They understood *menucha* as more than physical rest—it represents a positive state of peace, tranquility, and spiritual fulfillment.

This rabbinic insight transforms our understanding of Shabbat observance. True *menucha* is impossible when we're constantly checking our phones or scrolling through news feeds. These distractions prevent us from entering the spiritual promised land that Shabbat offers, where we can experience genuine rest for our souls.

---

1   Gerry Wagoner, Charlie Kirk And His Wife Begin Keeping the Sabbath, www.fulcrum7.com/news/2022/3/25/charlie-kirk-and-his-wife-begin-keeping-the-sabbath
2   Midrash Bereishit Rabbah 10:9 elaborates on *menucha* as a positive state of peace and tranquility.

Rabbi Abraham Joshua Heschel beautifully described the Shabbat as "a palace in time" - a sanctuary we enter not by changing our location but by changing our relationship with time itself. When we disconnect from our devices, we step into this palace. We free ourselves from the constant stream of alerts and updates, allowing us to experience time as a gift in which we can truly be present.

While the traditional Jewish observance of Shabbat involves complete abstention from all electronic devices for 25 hours, even a partial disconnection can be transformative. Here are some practical suggestions:

Start the evening before. Don't wait until Saturday morning to begin disconnecting. Set aside Friday evening as a time to begin winding down. Turn off notifications, close work-related apps, and begin transitioning into Shabbat mode.

Create a dedicated space for your devices. Like Charlie Kirk's drawer, designate a specific place where phones and tablets will "rest" during the Shabbat. This physical separation helps create mental separation.

Prepare alternatives in advance. Without our usual technological entertainment, we need other ways to spend our time. Stock up on books, prepare board games, plan walks, or arrange visits with friends and family.

Make it a family practice. When everyone participates in disconnecting, it becomes easier and more meaningful. Use the time usually spent on devices for family meals, conversations, and activities.

Don't feel guilty about rest. Many people feel anxious about being unreachable or "unproductive." Remember that rest itself is productive - it was commanded by God Himself as essential for human flourishing.

People who embrace this practice report surprising benefits. Without the constant interruption of devices, conversations become deeper. Without the pressure to document everything for social media, experiences become more authentic. Without the endless scroll of news and updates, our thoughts can turn to higher things.

Many find that after the initial discomfort passes, Shabbat becomes the day they most anticipate - a weekly opportunity to remember that we are human beings, not human doings.

Finding Joy Beyond Work and Commerce

What do you do when you can't work, shop, or scroll through social media? For many people today, this question reveals how much of our lives revolves around commerce and productivity. Shabbat invites us to rediscover the profound pleasures that money can't buy and technology can't provide.

The prophet Isaiah offers a beautiful vision of what Shabbat can be when we step away from commerce and work. He says: "If you turn back your foot from Shabbat, from doing your pleasure on my holy day, and call Shabbat a delight... if you honor it, not going your own ways, or seeking your own pleasure, or talking idly; then you shall take delight in the Lord" (Isaiah 58:13-14).[3] This passage suggests that by stepping back from our usual pursuits, we create space for a higher form of living.

Perhaps the greatest gift of Shabbat is the opportunity to simply be present - with ourselves, with our loved ones, with God. Without phones at the table or the pressure to rush off to the next appointment, Shabbat meals can become occasions for rich, meaningful conversation. Many families find these meals become a time for sharing the week's experiences, discussing ideas that inspire them, telling family stories, and passing down traditions. The simple act of catching up on each others' lives without distraction can be incredibly meaningful.

Shabbat is also an ideal time for the kind of deep reading that's

---

3   These verses establish the biblical basis for refraining from commercial activities and pursuing personal business on Shabbat.

hard to manage during the busy week. Many people keep special books just for Shabbat reading—not just religious texts, but any enriching literature that elevates the mind and spirit. Without the constant interruption of notifications and calls, it becomes possible to immerse oneself in ideas and stories in a way that's increasingly rare in modern life. Recognizing this, thousands of people have joined I Read This Over Shabbat,[4] an online book club where people discuss the books they read over Shabbat.

A Shabbat walk can become a form of worship when we take time to notice the beauty of creation. Whether in a park, by the ocean, or just around the neighborhood, walking without phones or other distractions allows us to appreciate what the Psalmist meant when he wrote, "The heavens declare the glory of God, and the sky above proclaims his handiwork" (Psalm 19:1).

In our productivity-obsessed culture, simple pleasures like board games, card games, and puzzles might seem old-fashioned. Yet on the Shabbat, these activities take on new life when we're not competing with screens for attention. They create natural opportunities for interaction and relationship-building. Even napping, often seen as lazy in our culture, becomes meaningful on Shabbat - a way of declaring that our worth doesn't depend on constant activity. The key is finding activities that help you and your family experience the day as a delight rather than a burden.

Shabbat is also an ideal time for hospitality - inviting others to share a meal, a conversation, or simply time together. This practice has deep biblical roots; Abraham himself was known for his hospitality, and the sharing of meals has always been central to building community. In our increasingly isolated society, the simple act of sharing unhurried time with others can be life changing.

Most importantly, Shabbat teaches us to appreciate simplicity. Joy doesn't require constant stimulation or consumption. Sometimes the simplest pleasures - a quiet conversation,

---

4   https://18forty.org/magazines/shabbos-reads/

a peaceful walk, an unhurried meal - can be the most satisfying. While Shabbat observance involves refraining from certain activities, its purpose is not restriction but liberation. By stepping away from the realm of buying and selling, doing and making, we create space for being and becoming. We remember that our value doesn't come from what we produce or consume, but from who we are as children of God.

As one rabbi beautifully expressed it: "During the week, we struggle to make a living. On Shabbat, we remember how to make a life."

The Shabbat Day Meal

The Shabbat Day meal is a perfect opportunity to connect with others. Just as we welcome the Shabbat with a festive dinner on Friday night, the daytime meal allows us to continue experiencing the joy and holiness of this sacred day. Traditionally, the meal is eaten a little bit earlier than a typical lunch to allow time for a third meal later in the afternoon. Many families invite guests and linger over this meal for hours, using the unhurried time for deep conversation and connection.

Like the Friday night dinner, the Shabbat lunch begins with *Kiddush,* sanctifying the day over a cup of wine or grape juice. The daytime *Kiddush* is typically shorter than the one recited on Friday night. As we do during the night meal, we then wash our hands and make a blessing over two loaves of bread, reminiscent of the manna which fell in a double portion on Friday. Traditional Shabbat lunch foods often include cholent or hamim - hot stews prepared before Shabbat and kept warm overnight, since cooking is not permitted for Jews on Shabbat itself.[5]

---

5   According to Jewish law, cooking on Shabbat is prohibited for Jews, as it falls under the category of melacha (forbidden creative work). However, this does not mean that observant Jews eat only cold food. To have hot meals on Shabbat, many use a blech (a metal sheet placed over a stove) or a crockpot left on before Shabbat begins, allowing food to stay warm without violating Jewish law. The popular cholent (in Ashkenazi communities) and hamim (in Sephardic communities) are slow-cooked stews that simmer overnight, ensuring a hot meal for Shabbat lunch.

The Shabbat Day *Kiddush*

Ve-shameru v'nei Yisrael et ha-Shabbat, la'asot et ha-Shabbat l'dorotam brit olam. Beini u-vein b'nei Yisrael ot hi l'olam, ki sheishet yamim asa Adonai et ha-shamayim v'et ha-aretz u'vayom ha-shevi'i shavat va-yinafash.

Zachor et yom ha-Shabbat l'kad'sho. Sheishet yamim ta'avod v'asita kol m'lachtecha. Ve-yom ha-shevi'i Shabbat la'Adonai Elohecha, lo ta'aseh kol m'lacha atah u-vincha u-vitecha avdecha v'amatecha v'hemtecha v'gercha asher b'sha'arecha. Ki sheishet yamim asa Adonai et ha-shamayim v'et ha-aretz et ha-yam v'et kol asher bam, va-yanach ba-yom ha-shevi'i.

Al ken beirach Adonai et yom ha-Shabbat va-y'kad'sheihu. Savri maranan v'rabanan v'rabotai: Baruch atah Adonai, Eloheinu Melech ha-olam, borei p'ri ha-gafen.

English:

The children of Israel should keep Shabbat, observing Shabbat throughout their generations, as an everlasting covenant. It is a sign between Me and the children of Israel forever, that in six days God made the heavens and the earth, and that on the seventh day He was finished and He rested.

Remember Shabbat to keep it holy. You should labor for six days and do all your work, but the seventh day is Shabbat for the Lord your God. You may not do any creative work - neither you, your son, your daughter, your male or female worker, your animal, nor the stranger who dwells among you. Because it was in six days that God made the heavens and the earth, the sea and all that they contain, and He rested on the seventh day.

Therefore God blessed Shabbat and made it holy. With the permission of the distinguished people present: Blessed are you God, King of the Universe, Creator of the fruit of the vine.

Zemirot - Special Shabbat Songs

During the Shabbat day meals, families often break into song, their voices joining in traditional *Zemirot* - special Shabbat songs passed down through generations that celebrate the sanctity and delight of Shabbat. These melodies transform the meal into something sacred, creating memories that children carry with them throughout their entire lives.

Yom Zeh M'chubad (This Day is Honored)

This beloved song encourages us to honor the Shabbat, promising that God will generously reward our efforts to observe it properly.

Yom zeh mechubbad mikkol yamim, ki vo shavat tzur olamim.

Sheishet yamim ta'aseh melachtecha, veyom hashevi'i lelohecha, shabbat lo ta'aseh vo melachah, ki chol asah sheishet yamim. Yom zeh...

Rishon hu lemikra'ei kodesh, yom shabbaton yom shabbat kodesh, al kein kol ish beyeino yekaddesh, al shetei lechem yivtze'u temimim. Yom zeh...

Echol mashmannim sheteih mamtakkim, ki el yittein lechol bo deveikim, beeged lilbosh lechem chukkim, basar vedagim vechol mat'ammim. Yom zeh...

Lo techsar kol bo ve'achalta vesava'eta uveirachta et adonai elohecha asher ahavta, ki veirachcha mikkol ha'ammim. Yom zeh...

Hashamayim mesapperim kevodo, vegam ha'aretz male'ah chasdo,
re'u ki chol eilleh asetah yado, ki hu hatzur po'olo tamim. Yom zeh...

English:

This day is honored above all days, for on it the Creator of the world rested.

For six days you may do your work, but the seventh day is for your God. On the Shabbat, do not do any work on it, for all was made in six days. This day...

It is the first of the holy convocations, a day of rest, the holy Shabbat day. Therefore, every man shall sanctify it with wine, and break complete loaves of bread. This day...

Eat rich foods and drink sweet beverages, for God provides for all who cling to Him garments to wear and bread in abundance, meat, fish, and all delicacies. This day...

You will lack nothing on it, you shall eat and be satisfied and bless the Lord your God whom you love, for He has blessed you more than all nations. This day...

The heavens declare His glory, and the earth is filled with His kindness. See that all these were made by His hand, for He is the Rock; His work is perfect. This day...

 Scan Here to Hear this Song:
https://www.youtube.com/watch?v=ojGlPkm8bjk

Deror Yikra (Proclaim Freedom)

Written by the medieval poet Dunash ben Labrat, this powerful song connects Shabbat observance with both physical and spiritual freedom. Its name comes from Leviticus 25:10, where the words *u'kratem dror*, "you shall proclaim freedom," are used in the command to observe the Jubilee year - a time when slaves were freed and debts were forgiven.

The song's verses weave together themes of God's protection and love with calls for redemption. This reflects the Jewish understanding that Shabbat gives us a weekly taste of the World to Come, when all creation will experience perfect rest and freedom. Its themes of liberation remind us that Shabbat itself liberates us from the mundane concerns that often enslave us during the week.

Deror yikra levein im bat, veyintzarechem kemo vavat,
ne'im shimchem velo yushbat, shevu venuchu beyom shabbat.

Derosh navi ve'ulami, ve'ot yesha aseih immi,
neta sorek betoch karmi, she'eih shav'at benei ammi.

Deroch purah betoch batzerah, vegam bavel asher gaverah,
netotz tzarai be'af ve'evrah, shema koli beyom ekra.

Elohim tein bammidbar har, hadas shittah berosh tidhar,
velammazhir velannizhar, shelomim tein kemei nahar.

Hadoch kamai el kanna, bemog leivav uvammeginnah,
venarchiv peh unemallenah, leshoneinu lecha rinnah.

De'eih chochmah lenafshecha, vehi cheter leroshecha,
netzor mitzvat kedoshecha, shemor shabbat kodshecha.

English:

He shall proclaim freedom for man and woman, and protect them as the apple of the eye. Your reputation will be pleasant and will not cease, Rest and be content on the Shabbat day.

Seek my Temple and my Hall, and perform a sign of salvation for me. Plant a choice vine in my vineyard, Hear the cry of my people.

Tread the winepress in Bozrah, and also in Babylon, which had prevailed. Shatter my adversaries in anger and wrath, hear my voice on the day I call.

O God, let bloom on the desert-like mountain, myrtle, acacia, cypress, and box tree. And to the one who warns and is careful, grant peace like flowing water.

Trample my foes, O zealous God, with faint-heartedness and grief. We will widen our mouths and fill them, our tongues will sing songs of joy for You.

Let your soul know wisdom, for it is a crown for your head. Keep the commandments of your Holy One, observe your holy Shabbat.

 Scan Here to Hear this Song:
https://www.youtube.com/watch?v=5FNTAoYnY2o

The Shabbat day meal ends with the Grace After Meals,[6] fulfilling the biblical command to bless God after eating and feeling satisfied (Deuteronomy 8:10). The rest of the afternoon provides an opportunity to spend time with family, study God's word, or rest and relax.

---

6   See chapter 3 for the text of the Grace After Meals.

Sacred Study: Making Time for God's Word

"This Book of the Law shall not depart from your mouth, but you shall meditate on it day and night" (Joshua 1:8). While this biblical command applies throughout the week, Shabbat provides a unique opportunity for deep engagement with God's word. Free from work responsibilities and technological distractions, we can finally give Scripture the focused attention it deserves.

Despite his royal responsibilities, King David made time to study, declaring: "Oh, how I love Your law! It is my meditation all the day" (Psalm 119:97). Yet for most of us living in the modern world, prolonged Bible study during the workweek remains an aspiration rather than a reality. Emails demand responses, meetings fill our calendars, and family obligations consume our evenings. The Shabbat creates a precious oasis of time specifically set aside for spiritual growth through study.

One of the deepest ways we experience the delight of the Shabbat is through studying God's word without pressure or distraction. Study on the Shabbat takes many forms. Some people attend classes at their synagogue, while others study independently, often exploring the weekly Bible portion that is read in synagogues worldwide. Many families incorporate Bible study into their Shabbat meals, discussing the week's readings and their application to daily life. The key is that this study differs from our usual rushed reading – it becomes contemplative, unhurried, an opportunity to dive deep into meaning.

Shabbat study offers something our souls desperately need – the opportunity to reorient ourselves to the ultimate truth. Six days a week, we absorb messages from advertising, entertainment, and social media about what matters in life. The Shabbat gives us time to immerse ourselves in a different message, to remind ourselves of what is truly important.

Rabbi Kalonymus Kalman Shapira called upon his students to take full advantage of their leisure hours on Shabbat: "Why let

Shabbat go to waste? Form study groups for yourselves. Those who are capable can study together independently, while those who need guidance can study with a teacher who will teach them Scripture, biblical teachings, religious commentaries, and other sacred texts. No one should feel embarrassed to participate in such gatherings. What's truly shameful is to wander aimlessly and engage in idle talk throughout Shabbat, living like work animals who know nothing beyond labor and sustenance. Learning and understanding God's teachings, refining both body and soul through study—this is nothing to be ashamed of. If your friends ridicule you for this, don't be discouraged, for only a fool would be ashamed of such worthy efforts. All community members should join study groups on Shabbat, both young and old."[7]

The Jewish sage Ben Bag Bag said about the Bible: "Turn it and turn it again, for everything is in it."[8] Each time we return to study, we find new insights, new applications, and new understanding. This is especially true on Shabbat, when we can approach study not as another task to complete but as an opportunity for discovery.

Parents often find that Shabbat provides unique opportunities to share their faith with children through study. Without competition from screens or activities, children are more receptive to learning. The relaxed atmosphere allows for questions and discussions that might not happen during the week. These study sessions become precious moments of transmission, passing the wisdom of the Bible from one generation to the next.

Even for those new to Bible study, Shabbat offers a perfect starting point. There's no pressure to cover a certain amount of material or reach specific conclusions. The day invites us simply to engage with the text, to let its wisdom gradually unfold in our understanding. As we make this practice regular, we find ourselves growing in knowledge and insight week by week.

7   Rabbi Kalonymus Kalman Shapira, Derech HaMelech, Sermons from Shabbat Shuva.
8   Ethics of the Fathers, 5:22

The prophet Amos foresaw a time when there would be "a famine in the land, not a famine of bread, nor a thirst for water, but of hearing the words of the Lord" (Amos 8:11). In our information-saturated age, this famine takes the form not of lack of access to God's word, but of lack of time and attention to truly absorb it. Shabbat stands as a weekly remedy for this spiritual famine, offering sacred time for the study and contemplation our souls require.

The Afternoon Prayers

Between meals, games, naps, walks, and Torah study, we also find time to pray the afternoon prayer. The afternoon prayer service, known in Hebrew as Mincha, holds a unique spiritual significance in Jewish tradition. The Mincha service is prayed daily, but on Shabbat it takes on additional meaning and depth.

The practice of afternoon prayer traces back to Isaac, as we read in Genesis 24:63: "And Isaac went out to meditate in the field toward evening." The Sages understood this to mean that he went out to pray. Just as Isaac found the afternoon to be an especially potent time for spiritual connection, Jews throughout history have maintained the practice to pray in the afternoon.

The Sages teach that the afternoon hours, particularly on Shabbat, are a time of special divine favor and grace. As the Shabbat begins to wane, there is a unique opportunity to connect with God through prayer.

The central prayer of the afternoon service is the *Amidah*, also known as the Silent Prayer. While structurally similar to the morning *Amidah*, the afternoon prayer carries its own distinct spiritual energy. As the day begins to fade, we affirm God's oneness and unity - "Atah Echad" (You are One). This reminds us that all existence, both light and dark, emanates from the One God.

The *Amidah*: Shabbat Afternoon Blessing

Atah echad v'shimcha echad, umi k'amcha k'Yisrael goy echad ba'aretz. Tiferet g'dulah, va'ateret y'shuah, yom m'nuchah uk'dushah l'amcha natata. Avraham yagel, Yitzchak y'ranen, Ya'akov uvanav yanuchu vo.

M'nuchat ahavah un'davah, m'nuchat emet ve'emunah. M'nuchat shalom, hashket vavetach. M'nuchah sh'lemah she'atah rotzeh bah. Yakiru vanecha v'yed'u, ki me'itcha hi m'nuchatam, v'al m'nuchatam yakdishu et sh'mecha.

Eloheinu v'Elohei avoteinu, r'tzeh na bim'nuchateinu. Kad'sheinu b'mitzvotecha, v'ten chelkenu b'Toratecha. Sab'enu mituvecha, v'sam'chenu bishuatecha. V'taher libenu l'ovd'cha be'emet.

V'hanchilenu Adonai Eloheinu b'ahavah uv'ratzon Shabbat kodshecha. V'yanuchu vah Yisrael m'kad'shei sh'mecha. Baruch atah Adonai, m'kadesh haShabbat.

English:

You English:are One and Your Name is One; and who is like Your people Israel, a unique nation on earth? A glorious elevation and crown of salvation is this day of holy rest You have given to Your people. Abraham was glad, Isaac rejoiced, Jacob and his children rested on this day.

It is a day of rest granted with generous love, a rest born of true faith, a rest in peace and tranquility, in quietude and safety, a perfect rest in which You delight. May Your children understand and know that their rest comes from You, and through their rest may they honor Your Name.

Our God, and God of our ancestors, please accept our day of rest. Make us holy through Your commandments, and grant us our portion in Your teachings. Satisfy us with Your goodness, and gladden us with Your salvation. Purify our hearts so we may worship You truthfully.

Let us, our God, in Your love and grace, inherit Your holy Shabbat; and grant that Israel, who honors Your Name, may find rest. Blessed are You, who makes the Shabbat holy.

Unlike weekday afternoon services, on Shabbat afternoon we read once again from the Torah scroll. This custom was instituted by Moses while Israel wandered in the wilderness. The Talmud[9] explains that when Moses saw how the Israelites' spiritual connection weakened after going three days without Torah study, he instituted public Torah readings on Monday and Thursday mornings, and Shabbat afternoons. This schedule ensured that the people would never go more than three days without hearing words of Torah.

The Shabbat afternoon prayer service provides a powerful way to pause and reconnect spiritually before the holy day draws to a close. Rather than spending the afternoon napping or socializing exclusively, taking time to pray helps maintain the sanctity and elevated consciousness that Shabbat is meant to cultivate.

The rabbis teach that Moses passed away at the time of Mincha on Shabbat afternoon. This hints at the unique spiritual potential of this time - it represents a gateway between heaven and earth, an especially auspicious moment for prayer and contemplation.

---

9   *Baba Kama* 82a

CHAPTER 6

The Third Meal

T HERE IS A special time, just before nightfall on Saturday afternoon, that touches the soul in a unique way. The Sages teach that this hour - when the sun begins its descent and the holy day draws to its close - is the most blessed moment of the entire week. While Friday night shimmers with the joy of the sacred day's arrival, and Saturday morning radiates with the glory of worship and contemplation, these late afternoon hours have a different quality entirely - one of yearning, of spiritual intimacy, of not wanting to let go.

Picture a synagogue in pre-war Vilna, known as the "Jerusalem of Lithuania." The stone building has stood for centuries, its worn wooden benches holding generations of prayers. As Saturday afternoon progresses, the natural light begins to fade. No one will turn on electric lights - that would violate the Shabbat - so the gradual dimming creates its own atmosphere. The diminishing sunlight filters through old windows, casting long shadows across the prayer books. The air holds both the warmth of the day and a hint of evening's coolness.

Men in their black coats gather for the third Shabbat meal, some sitting at long wooden tables, others standing in small groups. They sway gently as they sing melodies that have been passed down through generations. These are not the joyous tunes of Friday night or the triumphant songs of Saturday morning. The melodies now are haunting, expressing a deep yearning for something beyond words. Some close their eyes as they sing, others gaze distantly, as if seeing something far away.

Children sit quietly with their parents, sensing that something special is happening even if they don't fully understand what. Some drift off to sleep in the peaceful atmosphere, while others watch wide-eyed, absorbing impressions that will stay with them for life. Even the most rambunctious children seem to settle into the gentle mood of these hours.

This scene played out weekly in thousands of communities across Eastern Europe, from humble villages to great cities. While the physical trappings might have varied - some synagogues grand and others simple - the essence remained the same. Whether in Poland or Hungary, Lithuania or Ukraine, Jews gathered to extend these precious moments as long as possible, knowing that soon they would have to return to the ordinary world of work and worry.

This twilight hour on Shabbat afternoon carries a singular quality that Jewish mystics have cherished through the ages. The Sages named it *"ra'ava d'ra'avin"* - the desire of all desires[1] - a time when prayers are especially powerful. While Friday night welcomes Shabbat and Saturday morning celebrates it fully, these final hours before sunset allow us to hold onto the peace of the day just a little longer, reluctant to let go as the regular week approaches once again.

The Nature of Sacred Yearning

The air in these twilight hours holds a romance all its own - not the bright romance of new love, but the deeper romance of yearning for something just out of reach.

---

1   The teaching about the special sanctity of this time appears in multiple rabbinic sources. See Zohar II:88b.

Rabbi Joseph B. Soloveitchik explained that there are two kinds of yearning. There is the yearning for something we once had and lost – like people who have been exiled longing for their homeland. Then there is the yearning for something we have never yet experienced but know in our souls must be possible – a perfected world, universal peace, the complete revelation of divine truth. The closing hours of Shabbat uniquely combine both these forms of yearning.[2]

The great Hasidic master Rabbi Nachman of Breslov taught that the yearning itself is holy. He pointed to King David's words in Psalm 84:3: "My soul yearns, indeed faints, for the courts of the Lord." This yearning is described in the *Yedid Nefesh* song traditionally sung at the third Shabbat meal, with the line "For I have yearned so long to see your luminescent power..." In this Hebrew text, the word for yearning appears twice - "*nichsof nichsafti.*"

Most sages interpreted this dual expression of longing to mean that the deepest spiritual life isn't about reaching a destination, but about nurturing an endless desire for closeness with God. It's similar to how a small child might ask for "more hugs, more hugs!" when being held by a loving parent. The soul likewise cries out for an ever-deeper connection with its divine source. Rabbi Nachman, however, offered a unique interpretation of the doubled wording as "I yearn to yearn"[3] - suggesting that the yearning *itself* is worth yearning for. These fading hours of Shabbat afternoon create the perfect setting for experiencing such sacred longing.

The mystics taught that as physical light diminishes, spiritual light can shine more brightly. Like stars that only become visible when darkness falls, certain spiritual realities become clearer as

---

2   Rabbi Joseph B. Soloveitchik, *U'Vikashtem Mi-sham*, in *Ish HaHalakha*
3   Rabbi Nachman of Breslov's teaching about yearning appears in *Likutei Moharan I:31*. His interpretation of *nichsof nichsafti* comes from his discussions of Psalm 84:3.

the day's brightness fades. The great 16th-century mystic Rabbi Isaac Luria taught that at this hour, the deepest divine mysteries are revealed to those who make themselves receptive.[4]

This is why, even today, Jews worldwide gather for the third Shabbat meal as afternoon shadows lengthen. In modern synagogues with electric lights, in homes with every comfort, people still seek to capture something of that twilight holiness their ancestors knew.

The gradual dimming of the light becomes a metaphor for Shabbat itself - something precious that we know we must eventually let go, but which we try to hold onto for just a few moments more. Like a beloved friend departing after a wonderful visit, we walk them slowly to the door, prolonging the goodbye, treasuring each remaining moment of connection.

Unlike the festive Friday night dinner or the abundant Shabbat lunch, the third meal is traditionally simple. Some bread, perhaps some fish or a light dish - the focus is not on physical pleasure but on extending these final precious moments of Shabbat peace. Many people eat slowly, lingering over each bite, reluctant to reach the meal's end which signals the approaching conclusion of Shabbat.

This meal often takes place in the synagogue itself, with the community gathered together. The atmosphere is unlike any other Jewish prayer service or meal. There is talking, yes, but it tends to be softer, more reflective. The songs are different too - not the joyous melodies of Friday night but haunting tunes that express longing for redemption.

Songs of the Soul: Melodies of Yearning

The songs sung during the third Shabbat meal are unlike any others. These melodies, filled with yearning for God, create the spiritual atmosphere that makes this time so unique.

One of the most beloved songs of this twilight hour is *Yedid Nefesh*, Beloved of the Soul. Written in the 16th century by

---

4   Rabbi Isaac Luria, *Pri Etz Chaim, Sha'ar HaShabbat*, Chapter 24

Rabbi Eliezer Azikri of Safed, its words express the soul's passionate longing for closeness with God. The Hebrew text, with its rich imagery of love and yearning, reads like a love song between the soul and its Creator.

The melody to which these words are traditionally sung builds slowly, like a wave gathering strength. It begins softly, almost hesitantly, then swells with increasing intensity, expressing both the pain of separation and the joy of anticipated reunion.

Yedid Nefesh - Beloved of the Soul

Yedid nefesh, av harachaman, m'shoch avdecha el r'tzonecha, yarutz avdecha k'mo ayal, yishtachaveh el mul hadarecha, ki ye'erav lo y'didutecha minofet tzuf v'chol ta'am.

Hadur na'eh ziv ha'olam, nafshi cholat ahavatecha, ana el na, r'fa na lah b'harot lah no'am zivecha, az titchazek v'titrapeh v'hayta lach simchat olam.

Vatik, yehemu rachamecha, v'chus na al ben ohavecha, ki zeh kamah nichsof nichsaf lirot b'tiferet uzecha, ana eli, machmad libi, chusha na, v'al titalam.

Higaleh na ufros chaviv alai et sukat sh'lomecha, ta'ir eretz mik'vodecha, nagilah v'nism'cha bach, maher ahuv ki va mo'ed v'choneni kimei olam.

English:

Soul's beloved, compassionate Father, draw Your servant to Your will. Would that Your servant would run like a deer, bowing before Your splendor. For Your friendship is sweeter than the dripping of the honeycomb and any taste.

Majestic, Beautiful, Radiance of the Universe, my soul is sick with love for You. Please, God, heal her now by showing her the pleasantness of Your radiance. Then she will be strengthened and healed, and eternal joy will be hers.

Ancient One, may Your mercies be aroused and please have pity on the child of Your beloved, for it is so long that I have yearned intensely to see the glory of Your strength. Please, my God, my heart's desire, hurry and do not hide.

Please reveal Yourself and spread upon me, my Beloved, the shelter of Your peace. Illuminate the earth with Your glory, that we may rejoice and be glad in You. Hurry, Beloved, for the appointed time has come, and show me grace as in days of old.

 Scan Here to Hear this Prayer:
https://www.youtube.com/watch?v=9cG8dD1yU2o

Another central text of this hour is Psalm 23, perhaps the most famous of all psalms. While these words are familiar to many, they take on new depth in the gathering dusk of Shabbat afternoon.

In many communities, this psalm is sung to a haunting melody - a tune expressing both complete trust and intense longing. The image of God as a shepherd leading His flock beside still waters resonates deeply at this hour, when daily activities have quieted and souls turn toward their Source.

In many synagogues, someone will begin singing *Mizmor L'David* (Psalm 23) just as the last rays of sunlight fade from the windows. The congregation joins in, voices harmonizing in the growing darkness. The melody seems to hold both sadness at Shabbat's impending departure and yearning for its eventual return.

Mizmor L'David - A Psalm of David

Mizmor l'David .Adonai ro'i lo echsar .Bin'ot deshe yarbitzeini al mei m'nuchot y'nahaleini .Nafshi y'shovev yancheini b'ma'aglei tzedek l'ma'an sh'mo .Gam ki eilech b'gei tzalmavet lo ira ra ki atah imadi shivt'cha umishantecha hemah y'nachamuni .Ta'aroch l'fanai shulchan neged tzor'rai dishanta vashemen roshi kosi r'vayah. Ach tov vachesed yird'funi kol y'mei chayai v'shavti b'veit Adonai l'orech yamim.

English:

The Lord is my shepherd; I shall not want. He makes me lie down in green pastures. He leads me beside still waters. He restores my soul. He leads me in paths of righteousness for His name's sake. Even though I walk through the valley of the shadow of death, I will fear no evil, for You are with me; Your rod and Your staff, they comfort me. You prepare a table before me in the presence of my enemies; You anoint my head with oil; my cup overflows. Surely goodness and mercy shall follow me all the days of my life, And I shall dwell in the house of the Lord forever.

 Scan Here to Hear this Prayer:
https://www.youtube.com/watch?v=fuBOiMkPF-s

The Hasidic tradition added its own unique songs to this time, many of them without words at all. These wordless melodies, called *niggunim*, often express what words cannot. One such *niggun*, attributed to Rabbi Nachman of Breslov, begins with a cry of longing that gradually transforms into a melody of quiet joy, as if enacting the soul's journey from separation to union with the Divine.

The Piaseczner Rebbe, Rabbi Kalonymus Kalman Shapira, captured the transformative power of singing during the third meal: "During the third meal, when you are sitting amongst the Hasidim, it is impossible not to feel anything. While you are sitting amongst your close friends, how is it possible that during at least one song, or even one verse, you do not feel the embers of your soul beginning to catch fire; how can you not begin to feel a little trembling in your limbs!? ... The third meal is not only a time of worry over our lowliness, but it is also a greatly uplifting time... your heart and your mind shake and tremble from the noisy crash of the waves of the divine chariot that pass through your soul."[5]

As shadows lengthen, the singing often becomes softer, more intimate. Some communities have the custom of singing each melody several times, each repetition reaching for a deeper level of meaning. The Baal Shem Tov (Rabbi Israel ben Eliezer), founder of the Hasidic movement, taught that when a melody is repeated three times with proper intention, it has the power to open the gates of heaven.[6]

The Three Meals: A Spiritual Progression

The Jewish mystical tradition teaches that each of the three Shabbat meals corresponds to a different spiritual reality, ascending in holiness like rungs on a ladder reaching toward heaven. In addition, each meal corresponds to one of the patriarchs,[7] creating a progression through increasingly deeper levels of divine intimacy. Friday night connects to Abraham, representing love and the initial joyous connection of betrothal, filled with warmth as families and communities welcome Shabbat together. Shabbat lunch corresponds to Isaac, embodying awe and the

---

5   Rabbi Kalonymus Kalman Shapira, *Hachsharat Avreichim*, Chapter 4
6   Ba'al Shem Tov, *Shivchei HaBesht*
7   Zohar II:88a-b

more established relationship of marriage, making it a time for serious Torah study and contemplation. The third meal, linked to Jacob, represents union - the quietest yet deepest connection.

The Baal Shem Tov expanded on this teaching with a striking metaphor. He compared the three Shabbat meals to three ways of experiencing love. Friday night is like the passionate love of newlyweds - full of joy and excitement, but still somewhat external. The daytime meal is like the comfortable love of a long-married couple - deep and stable, but perhaps lacking the intensity of first love. But the third meal represents the highest form of love - when two souls connect so deeply that words become unnecessary and silence itself becomes eloquent.[8]

Rabbi Nachman of Breslov taught that at this hour, heaven's gates of mercy are wide open, but we can only enter them by transcending our usual physical and mental limitations. Just as the sun's diminishing physical light creates a unique beauty at twilight, the fading of Shabbat creates an opportunity for extraordinary illumination.[9] The Hasidic masters taught extensively about these twilight moments. Rabbi Levi Yitzchak of Berditchev would often be moved to tears during the third meal, explaining that at this time he could actually taste the perfection that awaits the world in messianic times.[10]

This connection to the messianic future is not coincidental. The prophets described the messianic era as a time of "endless Shabbat." Just as twilight combines elements of both day and night, the third Shabbat meal combines elements of our present reality with hints of future perfection. This is why many of the songs sung at this time speak of redemption and the rebuilding of Jerusalem. The prophet Isaiah offered a vision of this era: "Your sun shall no more go down, neither shall your

---

8   Ba'al Shem Tov, *Keter Shem Tov*, section 397
9   Rabbi Nachman of Breslov, *Likutei Moharan* I:279
10 Rabbi Levi Yitzchak of Berditchev, *Kedushat Levi, Parshat Ki Tissa*

moon withdraw itself; for the Lord shall be your everlasting light" (Isaiah 60:20).

The growing darkness of the third meal serves an essential purpose. Just as the deepest moments of human intimacy often occur in darkness, when external distractions fade away, the dimming light creates space for unprecedented closeness with the Divine. The mystics speak of achieving *naychah* - a state of deep, transcendent ease - during the third meal. After experiencing the fullness of Shabbat, it is possible to reach a clear recognition of the world's divine unity. This peaceful state creates optimal conditions for elevation. Yet paradoxically, this very tranquility exists alongside an intense yearning for even greater closeness with God. This state resembles that of a prince spending final precious moments with his father before a long separation.

This transition out of Shabbat can be spiritually precarious. The fall from such heights of holiness back into ordinary time requires preparation and protection. This is why the *Havdalah* ceremony is so essential - it helps us make this transition gradually and intentionally, carrying something of Shabbat's light into the week ahead. The spices we use are meant to revive our souls as the extra measure of holiness departs. But the yearning we've experienced in these twilight hours remains with us, informing how we enter the new week.

CHAPTER 7

Havdalah - Concluding Shabbat

I N THE NARROW streets of 16th century Safed, as darkness fully enveloped the hillside town, Rabbi Isaac Luria and his disciples would gather in the courtyard of their synagogue for *Havdalah*. By the light of a braided candle, they marked the departure of Shabbat with quiet reverence. Wine glistened in a silver cup, spices passed from hand to hand, and the ancient words separating holy from ordinary echoed off stone walls.

This ceremony, practiced since ancient times, connected them to countless generations before. For Jews throughout history—whether in medieval Spain, Renaissance Italy, or the shtetls of Eastern Europe—*Havdalah* provided not just closure to Shabbat but a moment to gather strength for the week ahead. Even today, IDF soldiers pause amidst conflict in Gaza or Lebanon to mark this transition with whatever they have at hand—perhaps a makeshift candle, a packet of spices, and grape juice instead of wine—carrying the peace of the day of rest into the harsh realities of war.

The word *Havdalah* means "separation" or "distinction," but this translation barely hints at its deeper meaning. This ceremony that marks the end of Shabbat is not merely a conclusion but a bridge between worlds - between the sacred and the ordinary, between rest and work, between the taste of future perfection we experience on Shabbat and the imperfect world as it currently is.

The Bible tells us that when God first created the universe, His first recorded act was one of separation: "And God separated between the light and the darkness" (Genesis 1:4). This divine act of separation continued throughout creation - separating the waters above from the waters below, separating dry land from the seas, separating day from night. The ability to make distinctions, to separate one thing from another, lies at the very heart of creation.

When we perform *Havdalah* at the end of Shabbat, we are, in a sense, reenacting this primal act of creation. Just as God brought order to the universe through separation, we bring order to time through distinguishing between the holy and the ordinary. The Bible commands us to "remember the Shabbat day to make it holy" (Exodus 20:8). The sages understood that this applies not only to Shabbat's beginning but also to its end - we must mark both with ceremony and significance.[1]

There is deep wisdom in this ritual of separation. Modern life tends to blur all distinctions - between work and rest, between holy and mundane, between public and private. We check work emails at the dinner table, scroll through social media during family time, carry our digital connections with us everywhere. The *Havdalah* ceremony teaches us the importance of maintaining boundaries, of acknowledging that different times call for different modes of being.

Yet *Havdalah* is more than just a boundary marker. The Sages taught that during Shabbat, each of us receives an additional soul, an expanded spiritual consciousness.[2] As the day departs,

---

1   This interpretation appears in the Babylonian Talmud, Shabbat 118b, where the sages derive from this verse the obligation to sanctify both the beginning and end of Shabbat.

2   This concept of the *neshamah yeteirah* (additional soul) appears in the Babylonian Talmud, Beitzah 16a. Rashi explains there that this extra soul brings expanded capacity for rest and joy.

this extra measure of holiness also departs. The *Havdalah* ceremony helps us transition gently from this elevated state back to ordinary consciousness. Like astronauts who must gradually decompress when returning from space, we need a careful process to return from the spiritual heights of Shabbat.

The timing of *Havdalah* itself is significant. It takes place not at sunset but after the appearance of three stars in the sky - when darkness has fully settled. Transitions between spiritual states require time. We don't rush from holiness back to ordinary life. We wait in the gathering darkness, allowing our eyes to adjust gradually to a different kind of light.

The ceremony uses multiple senses - taste (wine), smell (spices), sight (the flame), and hearing (the blessings) - teaching us that spiritual transitions affect our entire being. Each element carries deep symbolism: the wine represents joy, the spices console us for the departure of the Shabbat soul, and the flame reminds us of the first light of creation and humanity's first controlled use of fire, which according to tradition occurred as the first Shabbat ended.

These physical elements reveal how deeply we need physical actions to process spiritual transitions. Just as we need rituals to mark life transitions like marriages and funerals, we need a ritual to mark the transition out of sacred time. *Havdalah* gives us a structured way to hold both the sadness of the Shabbat's departure and the hope we carry into the new week.

The *Havdalah* ceremony reminds us that endings can be as holy as beginnings. While we naturally celebrate the start of things - the new year, the new month, the beginning of Shabbat - Judaism teaches us to sanctify conclusions as well. This is particularly important in our age, which often seems obsessed with novelty and beginnings while neglecting the sacred art of ending well.

Yet *Havdalah* is not just about ending Shabbat. It teaches us that true holiness lies not in permanently remaining in an elevated state, but in learning to move mindfully between different states of being, always maintaining our connection to the Divine while engaging fully with the world of action and creation.

The Elements of Havdalah: Wine, Spices, and Flame

The *Havdalah* ceremony uses four elements that engage all our senses, each carrying deep meaning: a cup of wine, fragrant spices, a candle, and the spoken blessings that bring them all together. Let's explore each element and its significance.

The Cup of Wine

We begin with a cup of wine (or grape juice), filled until it overflows into the saucer beneath. This overflow is intentional - it symbolizes our hope that the blessings of the coming week will be abundant, overflowing beyond the cup's capacity to contain them. The practice draws on the beautiful words of Psalm 23: "My cup runs over."

The wine serves another purpose as well. As we transition back to the working world, we need to remember that joy and delight are not limited to Shabbat. By tasting wine - traditionally a symbol of joy - at this moment, we carry some of Shabbat's sweetness with us into the week ahead.

The Fragrant Spices

Perhaps the most intriguing element of *Havdalah* is the use of sweet-smelling spices, called *besamim* in Hebrew. These might be cloves, cinnamon, bay leaves, or other aromatic spices, often held in a decorative spice box crafted specifically for this purpose. Some communities use fresh fragrant herbs or sweet-smelling flowers.

Why do we smell spices at this moment? The sages offer a

fascinating explanation. They teach that during Shabbat, each of us receives an additional soul - a heightened spiritual awareness and capacity for peace. When Shabbat departs, this extra soul departs as well. The sweet fragrance of the spices is meant to comfort and revive our spirits as we feel this loss.

Smell has a unique power to affect our emotions and consciousness. The fragrance of fresh-baked bread can transport us to childhood memories; a particular perfume might remind us of someone we love. By engaging our sense of smell at this sensitive moment of transition, the *Havdalah* ceremony acknowledges the deep connection between our physical and spiritual selves.

After the blessing over the spices is recited, the spices are passed around the circle of family and friends gathered, each person taking time to inhale their sweetness. This shared experience creates a moment of connection even as we prepare to go our separate ways into the new week.

The Candle

The most visually striking element of Havdalah is its special candle. Unlike the single-wick candles used to welcome Shabbat, the *Havdalah* candle must have at least two wicks,[3] and traditionally has several wicks braided together into a torch-like flame.

According to tradition, fire was the first thing God allowed humans to create for themselves. When the first Shabbat ended, Adam was afraid of the darkness. God then taught him how to strike stones together to create fire.[4] Thus, the *Havdalah* candle commemorates humanity's first creative act after the first Shabbat.

This symbolism runs deep. When we make the blessing over fire at *Havdalah*, as we begin a new week of work and creativity, we are not simply thanking God for fire - we are blessing God for the gift of human creativity itself. The fire represents

---

3   Shulchan Aruch, Orach Chaim 298:2.
4   Bereishit Rabbah 11:2 and Pesachim 54a.

all human inventions that have shaped civilization, from the wheel to modern smartphones. Through this blessing, we acknowledge that all human creativity and work can be sanctified and made holy when done for God's sake.

Like fire itself, which can both warm a home and burn it down, human creativity is a double-edged sword. Every major human invention carries this same duality - the potential for tremendous good and the capacity for terrible destruction. We see this dramatically in modern technologies, from nuclear power that can either provide clean energy or devastating weapons, to social media that can either connect or divide us.

The blessing over the fire at *Havdalah* thus becomes a moment of both gratitude and responsibility. As we prepare to re-enter the six days of creation and work, we acknowledge the gift of human creativity while also praying that we will use it wisely and for good. The light of the *Havdalah* candle reminds us that our creative powers must be guided by moral purpose. We pray that our innovations serve to heal and build rather than harm and destroy.

The multiple wicks serve several purposes. First, they create a more substantial light, which we need in order to fulfill the blessing's requirement to "benefit from the light" - traditionally done by holding up our hands and looking at our fingernails in the candle's light. The multiple wicks symbolize the diverse aspects of our lives that were temporarily set aside during Shabbat but now must be reintegrated. As the separate strands unite to form one flame, we prepare to bring the peace of Shabbat into the complexity of our weekday existence.

After the ceremony, some people have the custom of dipping their fingertips in the wine that has extinguished the candle and touching them to their eyes - a symbolic way of expressing our hope that the light of Shabbat will continue to influence how we see the world in the week ahead.[5]

---

5   Mishnah Berurah 296:1.

The Havdalah Ceremony: Text and Guide

Below you will find step-by-step instructions for the *Havdalah* ceremony that concludes Shabbat, including the full Hebrew text (in English transliteration), English translations, and practical guidance. While this ceremony has deep roots in Jewish tradition, its elements are drawn directly from biblical concepts and verses. The multiple blessings remind us of God's role in creating distinctions, as described in Genesis 1, and help us transition mindfully from sacred time back to our regular weekly activities.

What You'll Need

- A cup of wine or grape juice
- A spice box (*besamim*) containing fragrant spices (traditionally cloves and/or cinnamon)
- A special *Havdalah* candle with multiple wicks
- A small plate to catch wine drops

The Ceremony

Begin by filling the wine cup until it overflows slightly onto the plate below (symbolizing abundance for the coming week).

Opening Verses

Hinei El yeshuati, evtach v'lo efchad Ki ozi v'zimrat Yah Adonai, vay'hi li lishuah Ush'avtem mayim b'sason, mi-ma'aynei ha-yeshuah L'Adonai ha-yeshuah, al amcha virchatecha selah Adonai tz'vaot imanu, misgav lanu Elohei Ya'akov selah Adonai tz'vaot, ashrei adam boteach bach Adonai hoshiah, ha-melech ya'aneinu v'yom koreinu La-Yehudim hayta orah v'simcha v'sason vikar, kein tihyeh lanu Kos yeshuot esa, uv'sheim Adonai ekra

Behold, God is my salvation, I shall trust and not fear For God is my strength and my praise, and He has become my salvation You shall draw water with joy from the wells of salvation Salvation belongs to God; may Your blessing be upon Your people, Selah The Lord of Hosts is with us, the God of Jacob is our fortress,

Selah Lord of Hosts, happy is the person who trusts in You Lord save us; may the King answer us on the day we call The Jews had light and gladness, joy and honor - so may it be for us I will lift the cup of salvation, and call upon the name of the Lord

The Blessing Over Wine

Lift the wine cup and recite:

Baruch atah Adonai, Eloheinu melech ha'olam, borei p'ri hagafen.

Blessed are You, Lord our God, King of the universe, Who creates the fruit of the vine.

The Blessing Over Spices

Lift the spice box and recite:

Baruch atah Adonai, Eloheinu melech ha'olam, borei minei v'samim.

Blessed are You, Lord our God, King of the universe, Who creates various kinds of spices.

Pass around the spice box for all to inhale its fragrance.

The Blessing Over Fire

Lift the Havdalah candle and recite:

Baruch atah Adonai, Eloheinu melech ha'olam, borei m'orei ha'esh.

Blessed are You, Lord our God, King of the universe, Who creates the lights of fire.

Hold up your hands toward the flame, with fingers curled inward, and look at your fingernails reflecting the light.

The Havdalah Blessing

Hold the wine cup and recite:

Baruch atah Adonai, Eloheinu melech ha'olam, hamavdil bein kodesh l'chol, Bein or l'choshech, bein Yisrael la'amim, Bein yom hash'vi'i l'sheshet y'mei hama'aseh. Baruch atah Adonai, hamavdil bein kodesh l'chol.

Blessed are You, Lord our God, King of the universe, Who distinguishes between sacred and ordinary, Between light and darkness, between Israel and the nations, Between the seventh day and the six working days. Blessed are You, Lord, Who distinguishes between sacred and ordinary.

Drink from the wine cup, then extinguish the Havdalah candle in the spilled wine on the plate.

 Scan Here to Hear this Prayer:
https://www.youtube.com/watch?v=5Y9jPvnV5B8

Traditional Saturday Night Songs

After *Havdalah*, it is customary to sing songs of hope and blessing for the coming week. These songs express hope for redemption and blessing in the week ahead. The first song invokes Elijah the prophet, who according to Jewish tradition will herald the messianic age. The second asks for God's blessings as we begin the new week.

Eliyahu HaNavi - Elijah the Prophet

Eliyahu hanavi, Eliyahu hatishbi Eliyahu, Eliyahu, Eliyahu hagiladi Bimheirah v'yameinu yavo eileinu Im mashiach ben David Im mashiach ben David

Elijah the prophet, Elijah the Tishbite Elijah, Elijah, Elijah the Gileadite May he come to us speedily in our days With the Messiah, son of David With the Messiah, son of David

 Scan Here to Hear this Song:
https://www.youtube.com/watch?v=RikRMlcF7io

HaMavdil - He Who Distinguishes

Hamavdil bein kodesh l'chol chatoteinu hu yimchol zareinu v'caspeinu yarbeh kachol v'kakochavim balailah

May He who distinguishes between holy and secular forgive our sins may He multiply our offspring and wealth like sand and like the stars at night

 Scan Here to Hear this Song:
https://www.youtube.com/watch?v=y1b8pBoj2-s

A Bridge Between Worlds

The *Havdalah* ceremony celebrates an essential Jewish wisdom: the holy and the everyday belong in relationship with each other. Though we treasure Shabbat's deep restfulness, we also welcome our return to a world where we can build, create, and transform. The word *Havdalah* itself—meaning "separation"—reminds us that clear boundaries between different parts of life give each the space it needs to thrive.

As you end Shabbat each week, consider the wisdom *Havdalah* offers. This ancient practice teaches us to mark boundaries between rest and work with intention. In our rushed world where days blur together, these few minutes help us acknowledge what we're leaving behind and what we're stepping into. Havdalah reminds us that transitions matter—that how we move between sacred and ordinary time shapes our experience of both.

Part Two

The Theology of Shabbat

CHAPTER 8

Sacred Pause: The Theology and Law of Shabbat Rest

Divine Rest and Human Imitation

Picture a highly successful CEO who has just completed a major company expansion. She's launched new products, opened new offices, and hired talented people. Now imagine her doing something unexpected: she calls a company-wide meeting, not to announce the next big initiative, but to recognize what they've built together. She closes the office early, hosts a celebration, and takes a rare weekend completely unplugged. It's not that she's run out of ideas or energy—she's actually at her strongest. She knows that without this moment of pause and appreciation, everything they've accomplished would feel incomplete, just another item on an endless checklist.

This image of purposeful rest helps us understand one of the Bible's most puzzling passages: "God blessed the seventh day and made it holy, because on it He rested from all His work which God had created" (Genesis 2:3). The puzzle lies in the obvious question: Why would an infinite, omnipotent God need to rest? As the prophet Isaiah reminds us, "The Creator of the ends of the earth neither faints nor grows weary" (Isaiah 40:28).[1]

God's rest wasn't a response to fatigue but a deliberate act of creation—creating the concept of completion, of appreciation, of holy pause. The Hebrew word used here for rest, *vayinafash*, shares its root with the word *nefesh*, meaning "soul." Our sages teach: "If the six days of creation gave the world its physical form, the seventh day gave it its soul."[2]

When we stop our constant doing, teaching, and fixing, we experience this deeper kind of rest—one that comes from being present and appreciating what is. Like our CEO who pauses to celebrate achievement rather than immediately launching the next project, we mirror God's rest after creation—not a rest born of exhaustion, but a divine moment of beholding and delighting in what was made.

During the week, we're all creators in our own spheres. A teacher shapes young minds, a cook transforms raw ingredients into nourishing meals, a programmer writes code that changes how people interact with technology. Shabbat requires us to periodically step back from all this creating and shaping, not because we're tired (though we might be), but because this sacred pause completes the picture.

This is what it means to imitate divine rest. Just as God demonstrated sovereignty over creation by voluntarily ceasing creative activity, we show that we're truly created in God's image by doing the same.

Shabbat turns our world's values upside down. Most cultures treat rest as a tool that serves work—a necessary break to make us more productive. But Shabbat reveals a startling truth: rest is not a means to better work; it is the goal of our work. The six days of creation point toward the seventh. Our

---

1   This apparent contradiction between God's rest and His tirelessness is addressed by numerous Jewish commentators, including Rashi (on Genesis 2:2) who explains that "rest" here means cessation from creation rather than recovery from fatigue.
2   Bereshit Rabbah 10:9

weekday productivity isn't an end in itself but preparation for Shabbat's sacred rest. This reversal challenges everything our achievement-obsessed world assumes. We don't rest so that we can work more effectively; we work so that we can enter the fullness of rest. Shabbat isn't just a day off; it's a taste of the world to come, the ultimate purpose for which everything else exists.

This vision of Shabbat transforms how we understand human dignity. If rest is the goal of creation, not merely a tool for better productivity, then people have worth beyond what they produce. In our achievement-driven culture, we often measure ourselves and others by output, efficiency, and results. But by commanding us to imitate divine rest, the Torah establishes a radically different measure of human worth.

For the person caught in the relentless cycle of professional burnout, Shabbat offers a revolutionary message: human value doesn't depend on productivity. Our worth isn't measured by what we accomplish but by our very existence as beings created in God's image.

True Shabbat rest can fundamentally change the family dynamic. Most families use weekends to catch up—homework, house projects, preparation for the coming week. But what if a family instead set aside hours where they simply exist together? No improving, no teaching, no fixing. Just enjoying one another's company. Even this brief taste of Shabbat could shift how family members view each other during the rest of the week—seeing each other as valuable not for what they do, but simply because they are.

This is what it means to imitate divine rest. It's not about collapsing from exhaustion but about stepping back on purpose. We stop working not because we've finished everything (we never will), but because stopping creates room for what matters most—thinking, appreciating what we have, and being fully present with others.

The Path to Holy Rest: Shabbat and Jewish Law

How do we actually achieve this holy rest? What specific actions allow us to mirror divine rest and enter this different dimension of time? The Torah doesn't leave us to figure this out on our own. It provides a detailed framework for Shabbat observance centered on the concept of *melacha*. This term is commonly translated as prohibited "work," but a more accurate understanding is "creative labor" or "purposeful creation."

Melacha doesn't prohibit effort or exertion—you can take a long walk on Shabbat—but rather activities that impose human creative will on the world. This distinction is crucial. You may carry a heavy chair across a room (physical exertion) but not flip a light switch (minimal physical effort but creates a significant change).

The Bible doesn't provide a detailed list of what activities count as prohibited work on Shabbat. However, the sages recognized a significant connection in the biblical text: the commandment to keep the Shabbat (Exodus 31:12-17) appears right before the instructions for building the Tabernacle (Exodus 35). This placement teaches that the same activities used to construct God's sanctuary were the ones we should refrain from on Shabbat. In other words, the work that built the sacred space of the Tabernacle is precisely what we pause from doing to create sacred time on Shabbat.[3]

Why the Tabernacle? Because it functioned as a microcosm of creation—a distillation of all energies and patterns found in the material world. The activities performed in constructing it mirror God's creative acts in forming the universe. Therefore, by refraining from these activities on Shabbat, we acknowledge God as the ultimate Creator.

Jewish tradition identifies 39 primary categories of creative work that are prohibited on Shabbat. These categories form the

---

3   Babylonian Talmud, Shabbat 49b

foundation of Shabbat observance and are derived from the work done to build the Tabernacle. Every prohibited activity on Shabbat relates to one of these categories or activities similar to them.

To understand this concept better, let's look at a few examples:

1. Planting and Cultivating: The prohibition on planting on Shabbat does not only forbid placing seeds in soil. It includes any action that promotes plant growth—watering, fertilizing, or pruning. By refraining from gardening on Shabbat, we acknowledge that growth ultimately comes from God, not human effort. The natural world thrived long before humans learned to cultivate it.

2. Sorting and Organizing: Think about how often you sort things: separating laundry, organizing papers, filtering emails, or even picking the ripe berries from a bowl of fruit. These activities impose our human preferences on the natural state of things. On Shabbat, we pause this urge to constantly sort and organize. Instead of trying to perfect our environment, we accept things as they are—a powerful practice in a world obsessed with optimization and efficiency.[4]

3. Writing and Recording: In ancient times, this meant creating permanent marks on parchment. Today, it extends to typing emails, texting, or posting on social media. All these actions leave lasting impressions that change the status of the medium. By stepping away from communication technologies for one day, we remind ourselves that not every thought needs immediate expression.

4. Creating Fire: This represents one of humanity's first technological achievements—harnessing and controlling natural forces. In modern life, this includes using electrical

---

4   The sorting prohibition (*borer*) teaches that on Shabbat, we pause our constant urge to organize and perfect our environment. While traditional Jewish law allows sorting for immediate use (like selecting food to eat right away), it prohibits organizing things for later use or using special sorting tools.

devices, which create microscopic sparks when circuits close. Our digital sabbatical acknowledges limits to human manipulation of the natural world.

What unites these seemingly unrelated activities is their transformative nature—they all impose human creative will on the world, changing it according to our design. When we cease from these actions, we temporarily surrender our role as creators and transformers. We acknowledge that the world existed before us and can continue without our constant intervention.

In addition to biblical commands and prohibitions, the sages enacted what are known as "rabbinic laws" to safeguard biblical commandments or to enhance Jewish life. The Bible itself commands us to "follow their teachings" (Deuteronomy 17:11), giving rabbinic legislation divine sanction. However, rabbinic laws are distinct from biblical ones and generally carry less severe consequences for violation.

For Shabbat, rabbinic laws include laws and rituals like *muktzeh*[5] (the prohibition against handling certain objects), the requirement to light Shabbat candles, and the obligation to recite *Kiddush* over wine on Shabbat morning. Though these laws are binding on all Jews, rabbinic authorities have some flexibility in applying these laws in cases of significant need or unusual circumstances.

Lastly, Jewish Shabbat practice also consists of *minhagim*, customs that have developed over time. The Hebrew word *minhag* shares its root with *manhig*, meaning "leader" or "guide," indicating that customs serve as pathways guiding us toward better fulfillment of both biblical and rabbinic law.

---

5   *Muktzeh* (literally "set aside") refers to objects that may not be moved on Shabbat, first discussed in Mishnah Shabbat 17:1-2. The basic categories include objects that have no permitted Shabbat use (like money), delicate items that might break (leading to repair, which is forbidden), and items primarily used for prohibited activities. The laws are codified in Shulchan Aruch, Orach Chaim 308-311, with the foundational principle that these restrictions help preserve the sanctity of Shabbat by preventing one from engaging in or thinking about weekday activities.

Shabbat customs vary widely between communities. Sephardic Jews may have different melodies for prayers than Ashkenazic Jews. Some communities eat fish at every Shabbat meal, while others do not. Most have the custom of wearing specific clothing for Shabbat, though the style of these garments varies by region and community.

Customs can evolve over time and differ between communities. Sometimes customs become so widespread and deeply rooted that they gain the force of rabbinic law[6]. However, even then, they retain more flexibility than biblical or original rabbinic laws. When someone moves to a new community, they may adopt the local customs while maintaining certain family traditions.

Biblical law, rabbinic law and customs combine to form the complete structure of Shabbat observance. Biblical law establishes the core framework and the unchanging foundation that connects every generation back to Mount Sinai. Rabbinic law provides essential safeguards and enrichments necessary to help us fulfill God's will. Customs enable each community to manifest these timeless principles in ways that resonate with their members. This three-tiered framework allows Judaism to remain both anchored in eternal truth and adaptable to different times and places.

In modern times, many Jews have questioned whether all these restrictions are truly necessary. They yearn for the spirituality of Shabbat without its laws. Yet both the Bible and the painful lessons of history prove this isn't possible.

Jewish tradition teaches that when God gave the Torah at Sinai, the words "zachor" (remember) and "shamor" (guard) were

---

6   The principle of "the customs of Israel becomes Torah" originates in the Jerusalem Talmud, Pesachim 4:1 and is developed in Tosafot (Menachot 20b). The binding nature of customs is discussed extensively in Responsa Rashba 1:253 and codified by Rabbi Moses Isserles in his glosses to Shulchan Aruch (Yoreh De'ah 376:4). The hierarchical relationship between custom and law is analyzed in detail by Rabbi Moses Sofer (Chatam Sofer, Orach Chaim 1:28).

miraculously pronounced simultaneously - something impossible for human speech. Authentic Shabbat observance requires both the spiritual-emotional dimension (*zachor*) and the legal-practical dimension (*shamor*) working together. Neither alone is sufficient.

Supreme Court Justice Louis Brandeis once wrote of visiting his traditionally observant uncle Louis Dembitz's Shabbat table, describing longingly the serenity and spirit he witnessed there. Brandeis wished for "such a day as well, but without the restrictions." Yet history has shown that without *shamor's* protective boundaries, *zachor's* spiritual uplift cannot be sustained. This was painfully demonstrated when the ironically named Conservative movement,[7] attempting to preserve Shabbat attendance by permitting driving to synagogue,[8] instead saw their connection to Shabbat gradually disappear entirely. When liberal Jewish movements abandoned Shabbat laws, they sowed the seeds of their movements' collapse.

From Temple to Synagogue: The Historical Evolution of Shabbat Worship

The way Jews have observed Shabbat has undergone remarkable transformations throughout history while maintaining its essential character as a day of rest and spiritual elevation. During the First Temple period (957-587 BCE), Shabbat observance centered around the magnificent Temple in Jerusalem. Every Shabbat, the priests would replace the showbread

---

7   Despite its name, the Jewish Conservative movement represents a liberal approach to Jewish law and tradition that emerged in the mid-19th century. The term "Conservative" was chosen to position the movement between Orthodox and Reform Judaism, though its interpretations and practices generally align with progressive rather than traditional Judaism.

8   The CJLS (Committee on Jewish Law and Standards) of the Conservative movement passed a landmark responsum in 1950 authored by Rabbis Morris Adler, Jacob Agus, and Theodore Friedman titled "A Responsum on the Sabbath" that permitted driving to synagogue on Shabbat. The document argued this was necessary to maintain Jewish communal life in suburban America, though it sparked significant controversy. See Proceedings of the Rabbinical Assembly Vol. 14 (1950), 112-137.

- twelve loaves that remained before God throughout the week, fulfilling the command in Leviticus 24:8: "Every Shabbat day he shall arrange it before the Lord continually; it is from the children of Israel, an everlasting covenant."

The Temple service on Shabbat included additional offerings beyond the daily sacrifices. Numbers 28:9-10 describes these special Shabbat offerings: "And on the Shabbat day, two male lambs in their first year, unblemished, and two tenth measures of fine flour mixed with oil as a meal offering, and its libation." These offerings marked Shabbat as distinct from weekdays and created a focal point for national worship.

The first major transformation in Shabbat observance occurred during the Babylonian exile (587-539 BCE), following the destruction of the First Temple. Cut off from the Temple, Jewish communities established local gathering places for prayer and Torah study - the first synagogues. The prophet Ezekiel's words, "Though I have removed them far away among the nations... yet I have been for them a small sanctuary" (Ezekiel 11:16), was understood by our Sages to refer to these synagogues and study houses.[9]

During this period, the practice of public Torah reading, first established by Moses, was revitalized. Ezra the Scribe formalized this practice upon his return to Jerusalem, reinstituting regular Torah readings on Mondays, Thursdays, and Shabbat. This schedule ensured that Jews would never go more than three days without hearing Torah, helping to maintain a spiritual connection even without the Temple service.

When the Second Temple was rebuilt (516 BCE - 70 CE), Jewish worship developed along two interconnected paths. The Temple

---

9   The Sages' interpretation appears in Babylonian Talmud, Megillah 29a, where Rabbi Isaac specifically connects Ezekiel 11:16 to synagogues and study houses (*batei knesiot* and *batei midrashot*). Archaeological evidence supports the development of Jewish communal prayer spaces during the Babylonian exile, notably the Al-Yahudu tablets which document Jewish community life in Babylon. The timeline is further corroborated by biblical sources including Ezekiel 8:1 and 14:1, which describe elders gathering during the exile.

in Jerusalem remained the central site for sacrificial offerings, while synagogues spread throughout the land of Israel and the Diaspora, creating a parallel framework for communal prayer. During this period, the Men of the Great Assembly established the foundational structure of the prayer service, composing core prayers and blessings that could be recited anywhere. They set the practice of praying three times daily, aligning these prayers with the daily Temple offerings, and included additional prayers on Shabbat to mirror the extra Temple sacrifices.[10]

After the destruction of the Second Temple in 70 CE, a profound transformation in Jewish worship became necessary. Without the Temple, the Sages at Yavneh, led by Rabbi Yochanan ben Zakkai, reshaped Judaism around prayer and Torah study as substitutes for the physical offerings. This shift drew inspiration from the prophet Hosea's words, "Let us render the offerings of our lips instead of bulls" (Hosea 14:3). They preserved the link to the Temple service by precisely aligning the prayer times with the sacrifices: morning prayers corresponded to the daily morning offering, afternoon prayers to the daily afternoon offering, evening prayers to the burning of sacrificial parts overnight, and additional prayers on Shabbat and holidays to the special offerings for those days.[11]

The structure of Shabbat prayer continued to develop throughout the Talmudic period. The Friday night service acquired special significance, with the addition of Psalms welcoming Shabbat (*Kabbalat Shabbat*) and the famous hymn *Lecha Dodi*

---

10 Babylonian Talmud, Berachot 33a. Traditional dating places this institution around 515-332 BCE.

11 This historical account comes primarily from Babylonian Talmud, Gittin 56a-b, which details Rabbi Yochanan ben Zakkai's escape from Jerusalem and establishment at Yavneh. The parallel between prayers and Temple offerings is outlined in Berachot 26b. The translation of Hosea 14:3 follows the rabbinic interpretation in Midrash Tehillim 17:4. Archaeological evidence from the Yavneh period, including synagogue remains, supports the historical transition from Temple to synagogue worship.

in the 16th century. The Shabbat morning service expanded to include readings from the Prophets (*Haftarah*) in addition to the Torah reading. Torah study became increasingly central to Shabbat observance. The practice of gathering for public study sessions between the afternoon and evening services became widespread, fulfilling the directive to make Shabbat a day of spiritual elevation through both prayer and study.

As synagogue worship developed, so did home observances. The Sages describe elaborate Shabbat meals with special foods, songs, and Torah discussions. The practice of reciting *Kiddush* over wine, while rooted in the biblical command to "remember the Shabbat day," took on fixed forms. Family rituals like blessing children on Friday night became standard practices, creating a beautiful synthesis between communal and home observance.

The basic structure of Shabbat worship established by the Sages remains intact today. However, recent centuries have seen the development of new customs enriching traditional observance. The rise of Hasidism in the 18th century introduced new melodies and approaches to prayer, and the growth of women's Bible education has led to increased women's learning programs.

Throughout all these changes, the essential elements of Shabbat observance - cessation from work, prayer, Torah study, and festive meals - have remained constant. The evolution of Shabbat worship from Temple-centered to synagogue-based observance stands as one of the great achievements in religious history. It enabled Judaism not only to survive the loss of its central sanctuary but to thrive, creating forms of worship that maintain connection with ancient tradition while meeting the spiritual needs of each generation.

Changing Technology, Unchanging Principles

Perhaps the most significant challenge to Shabbat observance in modern times has been the advent of electricity and digital technology. The Torah explicitly prohibits kindling fire on Shabbat: "You shall not kindle fire in any of your dwellings on the Shabbat day" (Exodus 35:3). This command seemed straightforward in biblical times - don't light fires on Shabbat. But with the advent of electricity, our Sages needed to determine how this ancient principle applies to modern technology.

After careful analysis, rabbinic authorities determined that using electrical devices on Shabbat violates the spirit and letter of Torah law in multiple ways. Creating an electrical current is analogous to kindling a fire - both involve creating a flow of energy that can produce light and heat. Additionally, completing an electrical circuit is a form of "building" or "completing," another category of creative work forbidden on Shabbat.[12]

This ruling has had profound implications for modern Shabbat observance. It means no television, no smartphones, no computers, and no switching lights on or off. While this might seem restrictive to some, it has proven to be one of the greatest gifts to modern Jewish life.

In our hyper-connected world, the inability to use electronic devices on Shabbat has preserved the day's essential character as a sanctuary in time. When we put away our phones for 25 hours, we rediscover what it means to be truly present. Conversations become deeper and more meaningful without digital distractions. Families connect face-to-face rather than screen-to-screen. Our minds can truly rest from the constant stimulation of modern life. We rediscover the joy of reading, singing, and simply being present with those around us.

What might have seemed like a restrictive ruling has become

---

12 This ruling draws from multiple rabbinic responsa, notably Rabbi Shlomo Zalman Auerbach's "Ma'orei Eish" (1935), which first comprehensively analyzed electricity in Jewish law. Additional foundational sources include the Chazon Ish (Rabbi Avraham Yeshaya Karelitz) in "Orach Chaim" 50:9 and Rabbi Moshe Feinstein in "Igrot Moshe" (Orach Chaim 4:84). The classification of electrical circuits as "boneh" originates in the Talmud's discussion of building in Tractate Shabbat 102b, though its application to electricity remains debated among contemporary authorities.

a vital protection of Shabbat's spirit in the digital age. The ancient wisdom that guided our Sages in applying Torah law to electricity has proven remarkably prescient in our digital age.

Rather than attempting to change the law to accommodate technology, Jewish communities developed innovative solutions that respect both the letter and spirit of Shabbat law. The development of timers allows lights and certain appliances to function automatically without human intervention. Modern manufacturers have created special "Shabbat modes" for appliances that avoid electrical state changes. Shabbat elevators, programmed to stop automatically at every floor, allow the elderly and disabled to attend synagogue services while respecting Shabbat restrictions.

These solutions demonstrate how modern innovation can enhance Shabbat observance without compromising its essential laws. They reflect the Jewish approach of using human ingenuity to facilitate observance rather than looking for ways around the law.

The prohibition against using electricity has preserved numerous aspects of Shabbat's sanctity beyond just "disconnecting." Prohibited from driving cars on Shabbat, traditional Jews must live within walking distance of synagogues, preserving the close-knit community life that has characterized Jewish existence for millennia. Without entertainment devices, families rediscover traditional Shabbat activities like singing *zemirot* (Shabbat songs), studying the Bible together, and spending quality time as a family.

As technology continues to advance, new questions constantly arise. Modern rabbis must grapple with devices that operate through indirect sensors, the implications of artificial intelligence systems, and the complexities of medical devices that use electricity in novel ways. Yet the principles that guided our Sages in addressing electricity remain relevant: preserve the spirit of Shabbat as a day of rest, avoid creative manipulation of the physical world, and maintain the distinction between holy and mundane time.

The success of traditional Shabbat observance in our digital age demonstrates the Torah's eternal wisdom. By following these ancient principles, we create a weekly oasis of genuine human connection and spiritual renewal.

What seemed at first like a challenge - applying ancient laws to modern technology - has proven to be a blessing. The inability to use electronic devices on Shabbat has preserved the day's essential character as a sanctuary in time, offering desperately needed respite from the constant demands of our digital world. In this way, the wisdom of our Sages in interpreting Torah law has not only maintained Shabbat's relevance but enhanced its importance for modern life.

The Framework for True Rest

By refraining from these creative activities, we create a clear boundary between ordinary time and Shabbat. This isn't a series of arbitrary prohibitions but a practical system that allows us to experience the deeper rest we discussed at the beginning of this chapter.

These boundaries serve a crucial purpose. When we set aside our role as creators and manipulators of the world, we make space for a different way of being—one focused on appreciation rather than improvement, on being rather than doing.

The prohibition against performing *melacha* on Shabbat applies only to Jews. However, the underlying concept of setting aside creative work for a day of rest can be meaningful for anyone. Even without observing all of the restrictions, one might choose to pause from certain forms of labor—such as disconnecting from digital devices, refraining from shopping, or setting aside home improvement projects. Even this partial practice can open a window into the deeper rest God modeled at creation, offering a glimpse of the freedom and perspective that come from relinquishing control and trusting that the world will continue without constant intervention

Consider how this works in practice. When we disconnect from our devices for 25 hours, we're freed from the constant demands of work and social media. When parents don't help with homework on Shabbat, they show their children that value doesn't come from achievement. By saying "no" to certain activities, we create room to say "yes" to others that often get crowded out—deep conversation, prayer, attentive reading, and simply being present with loved ones.

This Shabbat practice brings us full circle to where we began. Just as our CEO found completion through deliberate pause, we find our fulfillment not in endless productivity but in purposeful rest. By entering this biblical pattern, we demonstrate that we are truly created in God's image not only in our ability to create but also in our ability to rest—to step back, see that it is good, and simply delight in what exists.

CHAPTER 9

The Family Lifeline: Shabbat's Rescue Plan for the Digital Age

"It is not good for man to be alone."

T HESE SEVEN WORDS from Genesis 2:18 reveal something unexpected. Adam had everything we might imagine necessary for fulfillment—a perfect environment, meaningful work, and unhindered communion with the Creator. Yet despite this direct relationship with God, Adam's existence remained incomplete without human connection.

This moment in Genesis strikes at the heart of Jewish understanding about human nature. Unlike religious traditions that exalt celibacy or solitary spiritual practice, Judaism has always maintained that family life itself is a primary avenue for holiness. The Talmud states explicitly that "He who has no wife lives without joy, without blessing, and without goodness."[1] From its earliest texts, Judaism emphasized the spiritual importance of building a household and creating relationships. This commitment to family life shapes how Jews understand spiritual fulfillment.

---

1   Babylonian Talmud, Yevamot 62b

Shabbat embodies this commitment to family life. While other traditions might view solitary prayer or meditation as the purest form of spiritual practice, Judaism places the family at the heart of Shabbat observance. The Fourth Commandment itself makes this clear: "Remember Shabbat to keep it holy... you shall not do any work—you, your son or your daughter, your male or female servant, your livestock, or the stranger who is within your gates" (Exodus 20:8-10).[2] The commandment addresses the head of household but encompasses everyone under that roof.

For families in biblical Israel, this commandment marked a radical departure from surrounding cultures. In an agricultural society where missing even a single day of work could threaten survival, God ordained that every member of the household—from the head of family to the servants and even livestock—would cease labor simultaneously. Every seventh day, regardless of harvest seasons or pressing needs, families gathered together away from the fields, setting aside production to focus on connection. This weekly pause allowed families to relate to each other beyond their working roles, creating relationships that transcended daily labor.

Kedusha, the Hebrew word for holiness, is often misinterpreted. People frequently assume that holiness requires complete separation from ordinary family life—perhaps like a monk in solitary meditation or a mystic on a remote mountain retreat. But through the narratives of our patriarchs, the Bible teaches us something remarkably different. Jacob's story in Genesis is surprisingly mundane—filled with details about sibling relationships, building a large family, raising children, and earning a livelihood. Yet Jacob's life represents the essence of *kedusha*. He

---

2   The inclusion of the entire household in the commandment to observe Shabbat is unique among biblical laws. The Mechilta d'Rabbi Yishmael (Exodus 20:10) emphasizes that this teaches the responsibility of parents to ensure their entire household observes Shabbat.

showed us how holiness exists not apart from everyday family life but within it. Jacob elevated ordinary household experiences into spiritual opportunities of the highest order by building a family amid challenging circumstances while remaining faithful to God's covenant. True *kedusha*, authentic holiness, isn't found by escaping family life, but rather when we bring God's teachings into our households and treat each relationship as worthy of respect and dedication.

Even more explicitly, when God speaks of Abraham's righteousness He emphasizes family leadership: "For I have known him because he commands his sons and his household after him, that they should keep the way of the Lord to perform righteousness and justice, in order that the Lord bring upon Abraham that which He spoke concerning him" (Genesis 18:19). Here God reveals that He chose Abraham specifically because Abraham would teach his children to follow God's ways. Abraham's holiness wasn't separate from his family responsibilities—it existed because of them. In Abraham's household, *kedusha* emerged precisely when he transformed family life into a channel for divine teaching.

This vision of family life as sacred space finds expression in how we relate to one another on Shabbat. During the six days of the week, we all too often treat our loved ones as functional parts of our busy lives—children need to be driven to activities, spouses must coordinate schedules, meals become rushed affairs between commitments. The Jewish philosopher Martin Buber would characterize these as "I-It" relationships, where we interact with others based primarily on what they can do for us or what role they play. In contrast, Buber described "I-Thou" relationships, encounters where we meet others as complete persons, not defined by their usefulness or function. Buber argued that only in these "I-Thou" encounters do we truly meet not only the other person but glimpse the eternal Thou—God himself.[3] Shabbat is precisely the time when we make this shift—from seeing family members as functions to encountering them as full persons worthy of our complete attention and presence.

Modern attempts at "family time" rarely achieve what Shabbat accomplishes. Most scheduled family activities today remain firmly in the "I-It" realm. Family game night becomes another obligation to manage, another box to check. Shabbat, however, creates the conditions for genuine "I-Thou" encounters by removing distractions and creating a separate time where family members can truly see and hear one another.

Rabbi Jonathan Sacks once shared an encounter with a television producer visiting a Jewish school on Friday morning: "There she saw the children enacting in advance what they would see that evening around the family table. There were the five-year-old mother and father blessing the five-year-old children with the five-year-old grandparents looking on. She was fascinated by this whole institution, and she asked the children what they most enjoyed about the Shabbat. One five-year-old boy turned to her and said, 'It's the only night of the week when Daddy doesn't have to rush off.' As we walked away from the school when the filming was over, she turned to me and said, 'Chief Rabbi, that Shabbat of yours is saving their parents' marriages.'"[4]

Sacred Boundaries: How Jewish Law Protects Family Life

When the sages developed the detailed laws of Shabbat, they weren't creating arbitrary restrictions. Rather, they were building a practical framework that would ensure this sacred time actually strengthens family bonds. The entire system of rabbinic legislation around Shabbat revolves around creating

---

3   Martin Buber, *I and Thou* (1923)
4   Rabbi Jonathan Sacks, *Morality*, 73

the conditions for genuine connection—removing distractions, keeping family members physically close, and elevating ordinary activities into opportunities for holiness. The legal structure of Shabbat ensures Shabbat is not observed in isolation but within the embrace of family life.

The sages taught that Shabbat preparation is not just the responsibility of one family member but should engage the entire household. The Talmud paints a remarkable picture of how even the most respected and elderly sages participated in household tasks – Rabbi Safra would personally prepare meat, Rava would salt fish, and Rabbi Papa would fix lamp wicks.[5] These weren't just demonstrations of humility but examples of how Shabbat draws family members together in shared purpose. Even the most exalted scholars took part in these household preparations, showing that family bonding begins in the very act of preparing for the holy day.

At the core of this legal framework stands *Shalom Bayit*, "peace in the home"—a foundational theme that permeates all Shabbat practices. The lighting of Shabbat candles just before sunset on Friday evening is a perfect example. These candles serve a very practical purpose—they ensure that family members don't stumble in darkness and become irritable with one another. This simple act prevents the household conflicts that might arise from navigating a dark home.

The sages considered *Shalom Bayit* so essential that it outweighs other religious practices. If a family is too poor to afford both Shabbat candles and Hanukkah candles, the sages rule that they must purchase Shabbat candles and forgo the commandment to like Hanukkah candles.[6] Why? Hanukkah candles serve an outward-facing purpose—they're placed near windows or doorways specifically to publicize the miracle of

---

5   Babylonian Talmud, Shabbat 119a
6   Babylonian Talmud, Shabbat 23b

Hanukkah to the outside world. Yet Jewish law prioritizes the inward-focused Shabbat candles that maintain peace and harmony within the family home. Before we can hope to illuminate the broader world, we must first ensure that our own homes are filled with light.

The laws of *Techum Shabbat*, "Shabbat boundary," reinforce this idea. The sages set a 2,000-cubit limit (about 3/4 mile) on how far one may travel from an inhabited area on Shabbat.[7] While this might seem limiting to modern readers, the commentator Sforno explains that this boundary ensures families and communities stay in close proximity on the sacred day. Think about how different this is from our current tendency to scatter in different directions even on designated "family days."

Preserving Faith Across Generations

The Bible commands in striking language: "And you shall teach these words diligently to your children, speaking of them when you sit in your house, when you walk on the way, when you lie down and when you rise up" (Deuteronomy 6:7). Notice the emphasis - not just occasional teaching, but constant, natural instruction woven into daily life. Imagine a parent walking with their child, perhaps pointing out God's creation in the morning dew, or discussing divine providence while preparing for bed. This is the biblical model of education.

Mesorah—traditionally translated as "transmission" or "tradition"—goes far deeper than simply passing along customs. It is a living tradition that requires active engagement.[8]

---

7   The concept of *Techum Shabbat* is derived from Exodus 16:29, "Let everyone remain where he is; let no one leave his place on the seventh day." The specific measurement of 2,000 cubits comes from Numbers 35:5, which describes the area surrounding Levitical cities. The Talmud (Eruvin 51a) establishes this as the distance one may walk beyond the city limits on Shabbat.

8   The Hebrew word *mesorah* derives from the root m-s-r, meaning "to hand over" or "to transmit." This root appears in rabbinic literature in phrases like "*mosser l'talmido*," "transmitting to one's student."

Throughout Jewish history, we see this principle at work in fascinating ways. The Bible specifically instructs parents to expect and welcome questions from children. At Passover, for example, the Bible anticipates: "When your children ask you, 'What does this ceremony mean to you?' then tell them..." (Exodus 12:26-27). Notice how the question is not seen as a challenge to be deflected but as an opportunity for deeper understanding.

Annual festivals like Passover provide significant moments of religious transmission, but they prove insufficient for maintaining lasting religious identity when isolated from regular practice. Less observant Jewish families who limit their religious engagement to annual events like the Passover Seder rarely succeed in transmitting biblical values to their children. A once-yearly ritual, however meaningful, cannot withstand the constant cultural pressures of secular society. Shabbat, in contrast, offers a weekly structure for preserving faith and identity. The establishment of a non-negotiable weekly "appointment" with God and family—one that cannot be rescheduled or postponed except for genuine emergencies—creates the necessary frequency for effective transmission. The effectiveness of this model lies not in perfect observance but in consistent presence, creating a pattern that transforms religious identity from an occasional experience into a fundamental aspect of family life.

The Shabbat pattern has proved remarkably resilient and effective at transmitting tradition across centuries and continents. For Jews in 15th-century Spain, 19th-century Russia, and 20th-century America, the weekly rhythm of Shabbat created what sociologists might call "thick" religious identity - faith reinforced not just by beliefs or annual ceremonies but by regular, embodied practices shared with loved ones.[9]

---

9   The term "thick" religious identity derives from anthropologist Clifford Geertz's concept of "thick description" (*The Interpretation of Cultures*, 1973), later applied to religious studies. It refers to faith identity formed through regular embodied practices rather than abstract beliefs alone.

Annual festivals layer additional meanings onto the weekly foundation of Shabbat. Imagine a child experiencing the full sensory world of Shabbat each week—the taste of *challah*, the excitement of weekly Bible study with mom, the melody of family Shabbat songs, the touch of a parent's blessing on their head. Throughout the year, this weekly experience is complemented by the freedom narrative of Passover, the joy of *Sukkot* (the Feast of Tabernacles), or the awe of *Yom Kippur* (the Day of Atonement). Each festival adds new dimensions while reinforcing the basic pattern learned through Shabbat.

The biblical calendar should change the way we approach the challenge of passing faith to the next generation. Rather than asking "How do we make religion appealing to young people?"—a question that implicitly treats faith as a product to be marketed—we should ask "How do we create authentic family experiences that make faith a natural part of life?" The Bible's answer is clear: establish regular rhythms of holiness within the home. When families gather weekly around the Shabbat table, they create something that secular entertainment cannot provide—moments of genuine connection, love and joy that shape our children's identity for the rest of their lives.

CHAPTER 10

Queens, Bread, and Light: The Soul Behind the Ritual

BEYOND THE PRACTICAL observance of Shabbat lies a rich world of meaning. The rituals and customs aren't merely traditions to follow—they contain deeper lessons that have sustained Jewish spiritual life for generations.

This chapter examines the deeper meaning behind three key aspects of Shabbat: the dual imagery of Shabbat as bride and queen, the two loaves of *challah,* and the different lights that mark the beginning and end of the day. Each of these elements reveals something important about how Shabbat connects different parts of existence—bringing together the physical and spiritual, work and rest, the everyday and the sacred.

Shabbat as Queen and Bride

The ancient rabbis described Shabbat in language typically reserved for royalty and wedding celebrations. Rabbi Chanina would wrap himself in special garments on Friday evening and declare, "Come, let us go out to greet the Shabbat queen."[1] Another sage, Rabbi Yannai, would say "Enter, O bride, enter

---

1   Babylonian Talmud, Shabbat 119a

O bride."[2] These two images—Shabbat as queen and Shabbat as bride—are more than just poetic metaphors. They reflect a deeper reality, a different form of existence that we experience on Shabbat.

A queen brings order and purpose to her kingdom. She represents authority, dignity, and a higher standard of living. When we treat Shabbat as royalty, we acknowledge that this day stands apart from and above the other days. It orders our week, gives structure to our time, and elevates our existence above mere survival and productivity.

A bride represents relationship, covenant, and new beginnings. The wedding day transforms both parties into something they weren't before. By describing Shabbat as a bride, the rabbis were highlighting the intimate relationship this day creates between God and the Jewish people. Just as a marriage creates a new reality, Shabbat transforms ordinary time into something sacred.

An ancient teaching beautifully captures this reciprocal relationship. When God created the world, each day was paired with another - Sunday with Monday, Tuesday with Wednesday, and so forth. But Shabbat stood alone and complained to God, "Every day has a partner except for me!" God responded, "The Jewish people will be your partner."[3] In the same way that a people and their queen, or a bride and groom, form sacred bonds, Shabbat and the Jewish people sustain and elevate each other through their divine partnership.

These dual images transform how we approach Shabbat. Think of the excitement a groom feels when he finally sees his bride after six days apart. This isn't just relief—it's joyful anticipation, a moment he's been looking forward to all week. Similarly, Shabbat isn't merely a time to collapse from exhaustion,

2   Babylonian Talmud, Shabbat 119a. The Hebrew phrase is "Bo'i kallah, bo'i kallah."
3   Genesis Rabbah 11:8

but a reunion we eagerly await. The queen imagery reminds us that this day deserves preparation and reverence, not just passive acceptance. Together, these images teach us that Shabbat offers more than just the absence of work—it brings the presence of holiness, relationship, and joy into our lives. It's not just about escaping the daily grind, but about remembering what we're truly living for.

The Two Loaves: Remembering the Manna

The two loaves of *challah* on the Shabbat table might seem like a minor detail of the observance, but they hold a story far deeper than most realize. Those twin loaves connect us directly to one of the Bible's most remarkable accounts of divine provision—the miracle of manna in the wilderness. Behind this simple custom lies an ancient lesson about trust, preparation, and the delicate balance between work and rest.

When the Israelites were wandering in the desert after leaving Egypt, God provided them with a mysterious food called manna. "In the morning there was a layer of dew around the camp. When the layer of dew lifted, there on the surface of the wilderness was a fine flaky substance, as fine as frost on the ground" (Exodus 16:13-14). The people called it *man*, meaning "what is it?"—for they had never seen anything like it before.

This heavenly bread came with specific instructions. Each person was to gather only what they needed for that day—no more, no less. If anyone tried to hoard extra for the next day, it would spoil overnight. But there was one exception: "On the sixth day they gathered twice as much... two omers (portions) for each person" (Exodus 16:22). The double portion that fell on Friday would stay fresh through Shabbat.

At first glance, this appears to be merely a practical story about food distribution. But Jewish tradition recognizes that the manna narrative contains fundamental lessons about faith and work. The first lesson centers on trust. Each day, the Is-raelites could gather only what they needed for that day—no more, no less. They couldn't stockpile or ensure tomorrow's meal through extra work today. When some tried, the manna rotted overnight. This daily dependence taught them to trust God's ongoing care rather than their own ability to secure the future. How much of our anxiety and overwork today stems from the same impulse—a desperate attempt to control tomor-row rather than trusting God's provision? The Israelites learned this lesson one handful of manna at a time, and it remains just as challenging for us today as we try to balance diligent work with genuine trust.

Second, the double portion on Friday taught the importance of preparation. The Torah is specific about this: "On the sixth day, when they prepare what they bring in, it will be twice as much as they gather daily" (Exodus 16:5). This wasn't just a prac-tical arrangement but a spiritual principle. Moses explained to the people, "Tomorrow is a day of solemn rest, a holy Shabbat to the Lord'" (Exodus 16:23). The preparation for Shabbat—the gathering and baking in advance—was itself a sacred act. The Talmud teaches that one who toils on the eve of Shabbat will eat on Shabbat, connecting our preparation directly to our ability to enjoy the day's holiness. This is why Rabbi Shammai would buy something special for Shabbat whenever he found it, even early in the week, keeping his mind focused on the coming sacred day.[4]

These lessons speak directly to our modern condition. Many of us worry constantly about work and supporting our fami-lies. Our society encourages a mindset of scarcity—believing there's never enough time, money, or resources to go around. This drives us to check emails at midnight, sacrifice family time, and work ourselves to exhaustion.

---

4   Babylonian Talmud, Beitzah 16a

The manna story also challenges our modern obsession with accumulation. Think about what the Torah reports: "He who had gathered much had no excess, and he who had gathered little had no deficiency" (Exodus 16:18). When people tried hoarding extra manna, it rotted and bred worms. But the double portion stayed fresh through Shabbat, suggesting that when we work for the right reasons and honor sacred rest, we find a different kind of abundance—one that can't be measured in possessions or productivity.

The songwriter Tom Schiffour once said, "The past is irrelevant because it's gone; you're not gonna get that again. The future? That's all well and good but there's no guarantee for that. You get this one little thin slice of time called today. You get one slice of bread a day and you take that and you enjoy it. I just take the plain bread and whatever gets added to it is a blessing. But just the slice of bread itself is a great blessing."[5] This is the teaching of both the daily manna and the *challah* bread: learning to receive each day's blessing with thanks rather than anxiously grasping for more.

When we place two loaves on our Shabbat table, we're doing more than commemorating an ancient miracle. We're participating in an ongoing story about trust, preparation, and the sacred balance between doing and being. The act of eating itself becomes holy, transformed by intention and gratitude into a spiritual practice.

In a world of burnout and exhaustion, these ancient lessons about manna and meaning, about double portions and deep trust, speak more powerfully than ever. They remind us that we are not sustained by bread alone but by every word that proceeds from the mouth of God (Deuteronomy 8:3). They teach us that true security doesn't come from storing up treasure on

---

5   Tom Schiffour, A View From The Other Side of The Mountain, https://open.spotify.com/episode/1QYIxA7AWbXP3PnYvFV79t?si=5fgdleIITb6W96i_4XeXTg

earth but from learning to receive our daily bread with gratitude and trust.

Light and Darkness: The Theology of Shabbat Candles and Havdalah

Shabbat begins with the lighting of candles and concludes
with the distinctive flame of the *havdalah* ceremony. These two
rituals do more than simply mark time—they represent profound theological concepts about holiness, creation, and our
relationship with God.

"Let there be light" (Genesis 1:3) are the first words God
speaks in the Torah. The sages teach that this primordial light
was not ordinary physical light but a special spiritual illumination. Though this original divine light was later concealed,
reserved for the righteous in the world to come, we can still
experience echoes of it through our observance of Shabbat.

When a family gathers around the table before sunset on
Friday, lighting the Shabbat candles creates a moment of transition. Though we typically light two candles, representing the
dual commandments to "remember" and "observe" Shabbat
from Exodus and Deuteronomy, the blessing refers to *"ner shel
Shabbat"*—"the light of Shabbat" in the singular. This points to a
deeper unity: multiple physical flames but one spiritual purpose.

The soft glow of Shabbat candles transforms our perception.
In ordinary lighting, we see only surfaces—objects, tasks, distractions. Candlelight reveals depth, texture, and the faces of
loved ones in a new way. This connects to Isaiah's words: "The
people who walked in darkness have seen a great light" (Isaiah
9:1). Throughout the week, we move through life focused on
material concerns, but Shabbat illuminates what matters most.

The custom of covering one's eyes during the candle blessing has practical origins but contains profound symbolism.
When we uncover our eyes after the blessing, our first sight is

the Shabbat light—a moment of reorientation from everyday seeing to spiritual vision. This simple gesture marks our transition from *chol* (the ordinary) to *kodesh* (the sacred).

Twenty-five hours later, as three stars appear in the Saturday night sky, Shabbat concludes with a different kind of light. The *havdalah* ceremony features a special candle with multiple wicks woven together, creating a bright, distinctive flame unlike the separate, stationary Shabbat candles.

The term "havdalah" comes from the root b-d-l, meaning separation or distinction—the same root used in Genesis when God separates light from darkness (Genesis 1:4). Just as creation began with distinction, our week begins with ritual separation between sacred and ordinary time.

The contrast between these two ritual lights reveals their complementary purposes. Shabbat candles burn steadily, creating an atmosphere of peace and receptivity. The *havdalah* flame, bright and dynamic, prepares us for action and engagement. One helps us enter sacred time; the other helps us carry its inspiration into the ordinary world.

When we raise our hands to the *havdalah* flame, we're preparing to use these hands in the week ahead. Rabbi Levi Yitzchak of Berditchev teaches that this moment invites reflection: How will we bring Shabbat's values into our everyday actions? How will we use our creative abilities to elevate the mundane through *mitzvot* (commandments) and good deeds?[6]

This pattern—moving between rest and activity, between being and doing—mirrors the cosmic rhythm established at creation. We need both states: sometimes the gentle light of Shabbat candles helps us appreciate what's already present, while other times, we need the bright flame of *havdalah* to illuminate our path forward.

In our modern world dominated by the artificial light of

---

6   Rabbi Levi Yitzchak of Berditchev, *Kedushat Levi*, Havdalah

screens, these ritual lights offer a different quality of awareness. Digital light keeps us perpetually alert and stimulated, often disconnecting us from our surroundings. The ritual lights of Shabbat connect us—to God, to tradition, to loved ones, and to the present moment.

Through the holy discipline of lighting candles at the beginning of Shabbat and kindling the *havdalah* flame at its conclusion, we transform time itself. These acts are not merely symbolic gestures but concrete tools that shape our consciousness. The Shabbat candles command us to stop striving and recognize the inherent holiness already present in the world. The *havdalah* flame challenges us to carry that recognition into our creative endeavors during the six days of work. Together, they teach us that the highest spiritual achievement is not to escape the world but to move between sacred rest and purposeful action, between receiving God's gifts and partnering with God in ongoing creation.

CHAPTER 11

The Day and People that Refused to Die

I MAGINE YOURSELF IN Jerusalem in the year 30 BCE. The magnificent Second Temple, rebuilt by King Herod, dominates the city skyline. As Friday afternoon approaches, a silver trumpet sounds from the Temple Mount, signaling to the surrounding neighborhoods that Shabbat is approaching. Shopkeepers in the bustling marketplace begin closing their stalls. The water-drawer makes his final rounds, ensuring every home has enough water for Shabbat. In homes throughout the city, families are preparing. The distinctive aroma of a slow-cooked stew fills the narrow streets - this hearty dish will cook overnight to provide hot food for Shabbat lunch, since no cooking can be done on the holy day itself.

Fast forward several centuries to Babylon, around 500 CE. The Temple is long destroyed, but Jewish life flourishes in this new center. Here, the great academies that produced the Talmud are in full swing. On Shabbat, the streets of Jewish neighborhoods in cities like Pumbedita come alive with the sounds of Bible study. Families walk to the synagogue, where the weekly Torah portion is read from scrolls virtually identical to those we use today. The same prayers we still recite - the Friday night *Kiddush,* the Shabbat morning service - are already ancient traditions by this time.

Travel west to medieval Spain, circa 1100 CE. In cities like Toledo and Cordoba, Jews have achieved unprecedented prosperity under Muslim rule. Their homes are elegant, their dress sophisticated, but Shabbat remains their anchor. The great Jewish philosopher Maimonides wrote detailed instructions for Shabbat observance that are still followed today. In these communities, Shabbat tables are graced with both traditional Jewish dishes and local Spanish delicacies, showing how Jews maintained their distinct identity while engaging with the broader culture.

Not all periods were so golden. In medieval Christian Europe, Jews often lived in cramped ghettos, facing constant persecution. Yet even there - perhaps especially there - Shabbat gave the Jewish people strength. In the crowded Jewish quarter of Prague in the 1600s, families would pool their meager resources to ensure everyone had something special for Shabbat. The flickering Shabbat candles illuminated homes that were poor in material goods but rich in tradition and faith.

The story of Shabbat observance is inseparable from the epic journey of the Jewish people through history. When we look back through time - not hundreds but thousands of years - we find Jews in radically different circumstances all bound together by this unbreakable chain of tradition that transcends persecution, exile, and the passage of empires.

This consistency is remarkable. When Jews were lighting Shabbat candles in medieval Poland, much of Europe still clung to ancient pagan customs. When Jewish families were gathering for Shabbat meals in ancient Persia, Mohammed had not yet been born. When the first Jews began celebrating Shabbat in the Sinai desert, Rome wasn't even a village. Few human practices can claim such continuity—a weekly rhythm maintained across millennia while mighty empires rose and crumbled around it.

Jewish History: A Tale of Two Dispersions

To understand how Shabbat evolved across the Jewish world, we must first understand a pivotal chapter in Jewish history. In 70 CE, the Romans destroyed the Second Temple in Jerusalem and began exiling Jews from their homeland. This exile, or diaspora, sent Jewish communities in two main directions: some traveled through North Africa into Spain and Portugal, while others moved north through Italy into Central and Eastern Europe.

The Jews who settled in Spain, North Africa, and the Middle East became known as Sephardic Jews (from *"Sepharad,"* the Hebrew word for Spain). These communities flourished particularly during the Golden Age of Spain (approximately 900-1100 CE), when Jews lived under relatively tolerant Muslim rule. This period saw great achievements in Jewish scholarship, poetry, and philosophy.

In 1492, the story took another dramatic turn when Christian Spain expelled its Jewish population, bringing an abrupt end to centuries of Jewish cultural and intellectual flourishing. This expulsion came after years of escalating persecution under the Spanish Inquisition, established in 1478, which had already forced thousands of Jews to convert to Christianity or practice their faith in secret. Facing the terrible choice between conversion, death, or exile, approximately 200,000 Sephardic Jews fled Spain, scattering across the Mediterranean world and beyond. Many found refuge in more tolerant Muslim lands of North Africa, particularly Morocco and Tunisia. Others were welcomed by the Ottoman Empire, whose Sultan Bayezid II supposedly mocked Ferdinand of Spain's shortsightedness, saying, "You call Ferdinand a wise king, who impoverishes his country and enriches ours?" These exiled communities brought their distinctive liturgies, melodies, and customs to new homes in cities like Salonica, Istanbul, and Sarajevo. Some Sephardic Jews ventured even further, establishing thriving communities in Amsterdam, where they could finally practice openly again, and eventually reaching the distant shores of the Americas, bringing Sephardic traditions to the New World.

The Jews who settled in Central and Eastern Europe became known as Ashkenazic Jews (from the Hebrew word "*Ashkenaz*," which medieval Jews associated with Germany). Jewish communities first appeared along the Rhine River in cities like Mainz, Worms, and Speyer around the 10th century, gradually expanding eastward into Poland, Lithuania, Russia, and other Slavic lands. These communities developed under harsh circumstances, enduring waves of persecution triggered by the Crusades, the Black Death (when Jews were blamed for poisoning wells), and periodic blood libels. By the 16th century, as conditions in Western Europe deteriorated, Poland-Lithuania became the center of Ashkenazic life, with Jews granted relative autonomy through the Council of Four Lands, a remarkable system of Jewish self-government. Living primarily in market towns and villages called shtetls, Ashkenazic Jews developed distinctive cultural practices, including the Yiddish language, particular styles of dress, and unique culinary traditions. Despite—or perhaps because of—these challenges, Ashkenazic Judaism developed extraordinary intellectual traditions, including the acclaimed *yeshivot* (religious academies) of Lithuania and the mystical, populist Hasidic movement founded by the Ba'al Shem Tov in the 18th century. For these communities, Shabbat became not just a religious observance but the centerpiece of Jewish identity—a day when even the poorest Jew could feel like royalty, when the hardships of exile temporarily receded, and when the spiritual treasures of Judaism could be fully experienced.

While both Sephardic and Ashkenazic Jews observe the same Shabbat, honor the same Bible, and follow the same fundamental Jewish law, they developed distinct customs reflecting their different historical experiences and environments.

Take the Friday night meal: An Ashkenazic family might begin with gefilte fish - ground fish mixed with eggs and matzah meal, shaped into balls or patties and poached. This dish evolved in cold-climate Europe, where food was scarce and expensive. By grinding the fish and adding fillers, families could stretch this precious resource to feed everyone. The accompanying horseradish (*chrain* in Yiddish) reflects the Eastern European love of sharp, pungent flavors.

A Sephardic family, in contrast, might serve *chraime* - whole fish cooked in a spicy tomato sauce with hot peppers and Middle Eastern spices like cumin and paprika. This dish reflects the abundance of fresh fish in Mediterranean regions and the influence of Arabic cuisine. They might also serve dishes like *tfina* (a slow-cooked stew) in Morocco or *hamim* (the Sephardic equivalent of cholent) in other communities.

The differences extend to prayer melodies and liturgical poems. Ashkenazic Jews might sing "Lecha Dodi" (the 16th-century hymn welcoming Shabbat) to a gentle, contemplative tune, while Sephardic Jews often use more rhythmic, Middle Eastern-influenced melodies. Even the Hebrew pronunciation differs - Ashkenazic Jews traditionally pronounce certain vowels and consonants differently than Sephardic Jews, reflecting the influence of European languages versus Arabic.

Yet these differences exist within a framework of unity. Both traditions light candles before sunset on Friday, make *Kiddush* over wine, enjoy three festive meals, and refrain from work until nightfall on Saturday. Both see Shabbat as a sacred time of physical rest and spiritual renewal.

With the establishment of the State of Israel in 1948, these two branches of Judaism that had developed separately for nearly 2,000 years were dramatically reunited. In the early years, this reunion was not without challenges. Ashkenazic Jews, who initially dominated Israeli society and politics, sometimes viewed Sephardic customs as less sophisticated, while Sephardic Jews often felt marginalized in the new state. Yet over generations, this reunion has produced a beautiful and exciting reconnection of traditions. In Israeli neighborhoods today, an Ashkenazic family might adopt a Sephardic melody for *Lecha Dodi* while a Sephardic family might serve *kugel* alongside their traditional Moroccan *dafina*. Marriage between the communities has become commonplace, creating families that honor both heritages. This blending of customs represents not a dilution but an enrichment of Jewish tradition – a living demonstration of how Shabbat continues to evolve while maintaining its essential character across time and space.

Shabbat Under Persecution: A Legacy of Spiritual Resistance

The preservation of Shabbat through centuries required both dedication and ingenuity. When poverty made candles a luxury, families would save all week to afford them for Shabbat. The Hebrew phrase *"oneg Shabbat"* - "the joy of Shabbat" - took on deep meaning as Jews transformed even harsh circumstances through their Shabbat observance.

From biblical times, Jews found ways to observe Shabbat even in the most difficult circumstances. The sages say that Queen Esther, living in the palace of King Ahasuerus, used the seven handmaids assigned to her (Esther 2:9) to keep track of the days so she could observe Shabbat while concealing her Jewish identity.[1]

This pattern of hidden observance continued throughout

---

1   *Midrash Esther Rabbah* 2:11

history. During the Spanish Inquisition, secret Jews known as "marranos" would risk their lives to observe Shabbat. Unable to openly celebrate, they would place a clean tablecloth on the table Friday night, light candles in a hidden room, or simply eat a special meal - tiny acts of faith that kept their connection to Judaism alive. Some families maintained these customs for generations without even knowing why, only that it was "what our ancestors did."[2]

The legacy of spiritual resistance carried into modern times. Jewish immigrants to America often faced a grueling cycle of poverty when they refused Saturday work, losing their jobs every single week. Each Monday morning would begin with the desperate search for new employment, only to repeat the pattern when the next Shabbat arrived.

In the Soviet Union, where Judaism was systematically suppressed as part of state-enforced atheism, Shabbat observance became an act of profound spiritual resistance. Jews like Eliezer Nanas, sentenced to ten years in a Siberian labor camp for the "crime" of teaching Judaism to children in Moscow, refused to work on Shabbat despite the brutal consequences. When guards cut his food rations as punishment, leaving him to face starvation in the sub-zero Siberian climate, Nanas remained steadfast. His fellow prisoners called him "Subbota" (the Russian word for Shabbat) because of his unwavering commitment. Through an unexpected twist of fate involving the camp commander's daughter, who became fascinated with the Jewish understanding of the World to Come, Nanas eventually survived and made his way to Israel. Similar stories unfolded across the Soviet empire, where Jews would gather in secret, risking imprisonment to preserve their Shabbat traditions, often with nothing more than a small candle and a shared memory of prayers.

---

2   Even today, some descendants of secret Jews in Spain and Portugal still light candles in closets, cover their tables on Friday nights, or avoid eating pork, sometimes without knowing the origins of these practices. In recent years, some have rediscovered their Jewish heritage and returned to open observance.

Even in the Nazi concentration camps, where maintaining any Jewish practice could mean instant death, Jews found remarkable ways to observe Shabbat. Women in Auschwitz would save tiny scraps of margarine from their meager weekly rations, fashioning makeshift candles with threads pulled from their prison garments. One survivor recalled how her mother would cover her eyes over these barely visible flames and whisper the blessing, careful not to be heard by the guards. Others remembered Jews in Bergen-Belsen who would save a small piece of their bread all week—despite near-starvation—to have something special for Shabbat. In some barracks, someone who knew the prayers by heart would silently mouth the words while others gathered around, pretending to be engaged in permitted activities. In labor camps, Jews would deliberately slow their work pace on Shabbat when possible, a dangerous form of resistance that could result in beating or death if noticed. These small, hidden acts of devotion revealed the extraordinary depths of Jewish commitment to preserve what mattered most, even in humanity's darkest hour.

The legacy of Shabbat as spiritual resistance continues to our own day. On October 7, 2023, when Hamas terrorists attacked southern Israel, killing over 1,200 people and taking more than 240 hostages, 20-year-old Agam Berger was among those kidnapped. During her 484 days of captivity in Gaza, Agam refused to cook on Shabbat despite the desperate conditions. When finally rescued and handed a whiteboard in the Israeli military helicopter, she wrote: "I chose the path of faith, and in the path of faith I returned (based on Psalms 119:30)."

This commitment to faith extended to her entire family. Her mother Meirav, who had begun observing Shabbat just months before Agam's capture, maintained her dedication throughout the agonizing wait. When the possibility arose that Agam might be released on Shabbat, Meirav requested: "I will wait for Agam,

God willing, when she arrives, with as little desecration of the Shabbat as possible." She asked those supporting the hostages' families to avoid taking photos until after Shabbat ended. In what many saw as divine providence, while previous hostage releases had occurred on Shabbat, Agam was released on a Thursday, ensuring her reunion would not violate the holy day.

The Unbroken Chain Continues

Throughout Jewish history, Shabbat has remained the constant thread connecting generations across time and space. While empires rose and fell, while Jews were scattered across continents, this weekly practice endured. In Jerusalem's Old City today, the Friday afternoon rush to prepare for Shabbat differs little from scenes that played out thousands of years ago in the same streets. In Brooklyn apartments and Jerusalem homes, families light the same candles, recite the same blessings, and share the same rhythms that sustained their ancestors through the darkest periods of history.

What makes this continuity remarkable is its practical nature. Shabbat isn't merely an idea or a philosophy—it's something Jews do. The physical acts of lighting candles, blessing wine, breaking bread, and refraining from work create a tangible link to the past. A contemporary Jewish family sitting down to their Shabbat meal is not just reminded of history; they're reenacting it, participating in the same concrete practices that defined Jewish life for millennia.

This faithful preservation of Shabbat through catastrophes and centuries stands as a testament to Jewish memory and commitment. It reminds us that some things are worth keeping, regardless of convenience or changing times. In a world that increasingly values innovation over tradition, efficiency over meaning, and constant connectivity over deliberate rest, Shabbat offers a powerful counterwitness. It declares that holiness exists in time itself, that stepping away from creation can be as sacred as building it, and that an ancient practice can still answer modern hungers. As long as there are Jews, the candles will continue to be lit - and God's holy day will never be forgotten.

Shabbat Resistance: Fighting Back with Holy Time

BEGINNING SOMETHING NEW can feel overwhelming, especially when it involves changing established family routines. Yet the Bible teaches us that small beginnings should not be despised (Zechariah 4:10). Just as God created the world step by step over six days before resting on the seventh, the journey toward establishing a meaningful weekly rest can begin with small but intentional steps.

Ultimately, the heart of Shabbat is not found in a prescribed list of rituals or restrictions, but in creating holy time - a space in our week dedicated to rest, renewal, and deeper connection with God and family. While Jewish tradition has developed beautiful and meaningful ways to observe Shabbat over thousands of years, the core biblical principle of setting aside one day a week for rest and spiritual refreshment is a gift available to all humanity. God blessed the seventh day and made it holy long before the Jewish people even existed.

Standing Together: Jews and Christians in a Time of Crisis

Western civilization is lost and broken and desperately needs to reconnect with the wisdom and practice of the Bible. We live in an age of unprecedented connectivity yet increasing isolation, of remarkable productivity yet spiritual emptiness. The restoration of weekly sacred rest offers hope not just for individual families but for society itself.

But there's something even more urgent at stake. Today, Jews and Christians find themselves under siege in the modern world. The October 7, 2023 Hamas massacre of over 1,200 innocent Israelis - deliberately carried out on Simchat Torah, "The Joy of the Bible" - was not just an attack on Jews. It was the opening salvo in a war against all who hold the Bible sacred.

As the terrorists themselves have chillingly declared: "On Saturdays, we will murder the Jews. On Sundays, we will murder the Christians." This isn't merely rhetoric. The attack on Israel was a first step in their plan to defeat the God of Israel and all who believe in Him. Israel is first, but Europe and America are next.

What unites the strange alliance between Islamic jihadists and secular progressives? Despite their radically different worldviews, they share a common hatred of the Bible, Judeo-Christian values, and the people who live by God's word. As Psalm 2 describes, nations will "take counsel against the Lord" and seek to throw off the "cords" of God's law: "Let us break their bands and cast off their cords from us" (Psalm 2:1-3).

The enemies of Israel yearn to be free of these restrictions. Their primary goal in attacking Israel is their hatred for Israel's faith in God, the Bible and the commandments. Woke progressives view the Bible as the primary roadblock preventing them from fully implementing their secular worldview, while Islamic jihadists reject the God of the Bible, the God of morality and restraint.

We are in a world war over the Bible itself.[1] On one side are

---

1   See Elie Mischel, *The War Against the Bible: Ishmael, Esau and Israel at the End Times* (2024).

the jihadists and progressives who detest the God of Israel and the demands He makes upon humanity. On the other side are believing Jews and Christians - the "Bible people" who pledge allegiance to the God of Israel.

This war has forced people everywhere to choose a side. Every human being must decide if they will stand for or against the people of Israel, the God of Israel, and the Bible of Israel. There is no middle ground.

In this critical hour, the "Shabbat revolution" is our weekly declaration of war against those seeking to erase biblical values from our world. When Jews and Christians honor Shabbat, we declare our allegiance to the God of the Bible. Each Shabbat becomes an act of spiritual defiance - a declaration that we will not be swept away by the current of secularism or intimidated by the threats of jihadists.

Over the past century, Christians have gone from being the Jewish people's greatest oppressors to becoming their greatest friends. If in the past we clashed over our different interpretations of the Bible, today we recognize that it is the Hebrew Bible that binds us together and serves as the basis for our friendship.

We no longer have the luxury of arguing with one another about the Bible. When the final redemption arrives, everything will become clear. Until then, we must stand united with mutual respect, and fight, side by side, against those waging war on Israel, God, and the Bible.

The Prophetic Vision of Shabbat

The prophet Isaiah proclaimed a vision of the messianic age: "It shall come to pass in the latter days that the mountain of the house of the Lord shall be established... and all nations shall flow to it" (Isaiah 2:2). This vision of universal worship and peace is deeply connected to Shabbat's promise. When we observe the seventh day, we're not just following an ancient ritual – we're rehearsing for redemption, practicing for the world to come.

Imagine a world where Shabbat values spread beyond our homes and synagogues. Picture entire towns and cities keeping Shabbat, gathering together with their families on Friday night, faces illuminated by candlelight instead of screens. Children blessed by their parents. Songs rising from dinner tables. Stories of faith passed from one generation to the next.

The prophet Amos describes a time when "the mountains shall drip sweet wine, and all the hills shall flow with it" (Amos 9:13). This abundance isn't merely material – it reflects a spiritual reality that Shabbat helps us taste each week. The prophets Zechariah and Micah both envision a day when "everyone will sit under their own vine and fig tree, and no one will make them afraid" (Micah 4:4, Zechariah 3:10). This image of security, peace, and prosperity mirrors what we create in our homes each Shabbat.

The prophets of Israel envisioned a time when the practice of Shabbat would bring national healing and restoration. Isaiah proclaimed, "If you refrain from trampling the Shabbat... then you shall delight in the Lord, and I will make you ride upon the heights of the earth" (Isaiah 58:13-14). Through Jeremiah, God promised, "If you truly heed Me... to keep the Shabbat day holy... then there shall enter through the gates of this city kings and princes who sit on the throne of David" (Jeremiah 17:24-25).

This vision isn't utopian daydreaming. It's biblical reality. Throughout Scripture, Shabbat is the antidote to exile, the solution to spiritual crisis, the path back to God. When we keep Shabbat, Shabbat keeps us. This is what our world has forgotten, and this is what we, through our Shabbat Revolution, must restore. One family at a time. One dinner table at a time. One Shabbat at a time.

Shabbat Shalom!

Dedications

In July 2024, I experienced a profound spiritual awakening.
The message that resonated most deeply was simple yet
powerful: God loves everyone unconditionally. This universal
love is what we're all called to share with one another.
We all inhabit this world together, regardless of our differences.
May God bless us all on this journey.

Debora Van Landeghem

Dedicated to my father,

Don Wood Sr,

of blessed memory, who was my first teacher
about the uniqueness of the Jewish people.

Lori Hinze

Rabbi Elie Mischel's passion to educate and inspire readers while revealing prophecies deep within Scripture is astonishing with every book he writes. His newest, "Shabbat Revolution: A Practical Guide to Weekly Renewal" deepens our understanding of the Sabbath and empowers us with fresh Hebraic insights of what God's Fourth Commandment in Exodus 20 *really* means. The wisdom that Rabbi Elie so masterfully brings to this topic is the "link" that we Christians have been missing all along! This book is our invitation to sit at a round table and expand our knowledge, which will deepen our relationship with God. It is a universal invitation for Jews and non-Jews. So, pull yourself up to the table and be prepared to digest a feast in full-proportion from a God-centered perspective. ISAIAH 66:23 prophesied: "And New Moon after New Moon, And Sabbath after Sabbath, All flesh shall come to worship Me - said the LORD."

Debbie and Thomas Cope
Israel Liaisons - Christian Assembly of Schriever Louisiana

One does not have to be a Sabbatarian to appreciate the desperate need in our day for weekly Sabbath rests from the incessant siren call of doing. Drawing from biblical patterns and practices that have sustained spiritual life for millennia, Rabbi Mischel draws upon the rich history of the Jewish biblical Shabbat to awaken and enrich contemporary Christian's weekly experience with God in rest and renewal.

Pastor John Repsold

This is dedicated to all the Jewish people who have died
sanctifying the name of Hashem over the last 3,000 years.
May Hashem have their names recorded forever
in His book of remembrance.

Mark Biltz, El Shaddai Ministries

In memory of

Gladwyn Hay

one of the most beautiful souls ever created by
the God of the universe. How blessed was I to have your life
as a daily example and to be able to call you my Dad.
All my love and honor forever.

Trina Oshman

I dedicate this book to my son, Josiah,
daughters Lunda and Muchemwa
and my wife Patricia.

Ricky Bwalya

SPONSORED BY:

Sheri Salyer

Emilia Arredondo

David Johnde Liu

Lisa Preble

Martha Dever

Lisa An'Ne Dumon-Watson

Jim Pickett

Tami Podell

Dori Anne Rorabaugh

Bill Brady

Lee Johnson

Richard Bush

William Hardesty

Susan Blue

Jayne Foss

Robert Stys

Angie & Dean Cole

Manna Van Doorn

Marcus Hirsch

Shih Han Huang

Kristi Corey Ingram

Joanne Sanford Duke

Shih Han Huang

Hungwen Wang

Laura Davis

Keith Toogood

Maria Dodds

Michele Burke

Mitchell Harris

Joanne Sanford

Bertha Solomon Mathis

Amanda Faith

Maria Dodds

Bernard Leibtag

Janet Bazzone

Taimi Tellervo Rutz-Sanden

Debra Szentgyorgyi

Dennis Northington

Bible Plus

By **ISRAƐL365**

Study the Bible Like Never Before

Live Like David

Transform your daily spiritual practice with *Live Like David: Daily Devotional Journal,* an extraordinary three-volume masterwork that brings the timeless wisdom of King David into your daily life.

SCAN NOW!

Or visit israel365store.com